WOMEN AND WORK

WOMEN AND WORK:
Human Resource Management, Perspective

ANURADHA SHARMA

GYAN PUBLISHING HOUSE
NEW DELHI-110002

WOMEN AND WORK:
Human Resource Management, Perspective
[*Management, Sociology and Women's Studies*]

ISBN: 81-212-0627-8

Published in 1999 in India by
Gyan Publishing House
5, Ansari Road
New Delhi 110 002

Laser Typeset at Alphabet, Delhi
Printed at Mehra Offset Press, New Delhi.

Contents

Contents

PREFACE

'Women and Work' is an emerging aspect of Human Resource Management (HRM). Women will be the equal sharing workforce in the next century. Yet as a subject and field of knowledge the gendering issues in organizations have not received much systematic attention. This is also reflected by the fact that most of the management-theorizing about human resource issues appears ignoring the special needs and attributes of women at work. This realization in the recent years has brought about 'gender' as an important correlate of the work system. Some of the issues and major challenges of HRM are related to work motivation, designs of jobs, occupational choices, human resource development and impact of work-family interface in this theorizing. There is also a growing realization that 'women and work' have an additional dimension of 'home and family' and often women have to work harder to cope up with the multiple roles and demands. The existing HRM policies are gender neutral. However, this book attempts to present facts, figures and perceptions revealing that the world of work is different for men and women. Restructuring women's role is essential for allowing them to achieve excellence, competence and life satisfaction. Regardless of gender the organizations should attempt to discover the talents and creativity among the members of their workforce. There is also need to develop mindserian and egalitarian culture giving women opportunities for development. Even though Constitution of India provides equal opportunities for both the sexes, in practice discrimination against women are very common. There appears hardly any mechanism which could take immediate correctional action. Perhaps there is need for humanistic perspective in developing alternative paradigms of HRM.

This book is an outcome of the work carried out by the author and her convictions that there is no choice for us than to the develop new HR policies for the benefit of society at large. One of the major contributions of this book is the chapter on occupational choices and occupational patterns of women with science and technology education which is based on the results of a survey sponsored by the Department of Science and Technology, Govt. of India, New Delhi. The support of DST is gratefully acknowledged. Other reviews and studies have been conducted at the IIT Delhi. I am indebted to my Institute for all the support which I have received. I am grateful to the reviewers of the manuscript which has enhanced the quality of book and my colleagues in the Department of Humanities and Social Sciences and Management Studies for providing stimulating academic environment. Members of my family need special mention who allowed me to concentrate on my project without much expectations from me.

I hope the book will be useful for students, researchers and policy makers in the fields of HRM, gender studies and diversity at the place of work. I will certainly fed rewarded if any suggestion of this book is seen into action.

There is an urgent need to unfold the rudiments of micro level aspects of 'women and work'. This book has attempted to achieve this only in a limited way. The book is presented in eight chapters. These chapters relate to sociology, organizational psychology, and development aspects. These chapters have been organized as introduction discussing the HRM and entry of women as work partners followed by a discussion on work, gender and organizations. Indian work scenario is discussed next and it continues with a chapter on occupational choices of women with science and technology, education. Aspects of work design, motivation, personality, social justice and perception are discussed in the later part of the book. A brief analysis of reflection on human resource policies is presented in chapter. Finally looking ahead- futuristic perception emphasizing need for change in the management paradigm about the issue of women and work is presented.

Anuradha Sharma

ONE

Introduction

Human resources are foundations of organizations and play a key role in management of most capital assets. People are the most valuable resources of an organization.

Human resource management today emphasizes on employee's wisdom to gain competitive advantage. This approach emerges out of the organizational behaviour theory which suggests achieving performance and satisfaction by unfolding the skills, abilities and inner qualities of its employees. With the emergence of globalization and new economic order the issue of human resource has become pivotal for management studies.

Management of human resources involves several important and complex issues in the form of multidimensional reactions, involving employee's perceptions, personality, background, the objective realities of the organizational culture motivation, values leadership styles and intergroup relationship, to name a few, thus leading to employee's motivation for performance. This concept has changed drastically since the days of scientific management. Today the impact of modern behavioural sciences has given new insights to management of human resources. The management literature has also been greatly enriched by management philosophers, practitioners and researchers adding social, cultural, moral and value-based dimensions to the field.

One of the most important questions facing organizations today is the effective management of human resources. Although managers have always realized that there is some relationship among perception, motivation and employee's performance, it is only in recent years that these two concepts have started appearing as twins. The link among these factors involves a set of highly complex notions about the nature of employees and what motivates them to better job performance. There is, however, a growing realization that the employee today is indeed, a new breed with different values, needs, motivations, expectations and aspirations, than his predecessor. He is a product of knowledge explosion and the meanings of incentives appear to have changed—employee today is an increasingly matured, aware, creative and dedicated person on the job. As was believed earlier he does not seem to be impressed only by financial incentives. It is also observed that in spite of adequate incentives often motivation to better performance is still lacking.

The changing concepts about the management of organizations require a new look at the concept of 'motivation and performance'. If employees are motivated to work harder, better, with sincerity, initiative and cooperation, it will lead to competitive advantage for the organization and no amount of sophisticated technology or improved work method are substitutes to this human aspect. Every employee's satisfactory performance is vital to the proper functioning of machinery and equipment in an industry, and productivity is likely to be determined by what the employees do rather than the machines do, which in turn is also affected by diversity at the place of work.

Women constitute the new workforce in an organization and are entering into most of the professions. In fact they are the workforce of future India, taking equal share of responsibilities like men. Even though the importance of gender at workplace is not considered as an important aspect of human resource management by most people, this is gradually creeping into the world of work, which calls for an understanding of the gender processes and gendered practices in organization. It is being realized that in spite of cultural roots of gender hierarchies, women make a mark in their performance. Therefore, this area of human resource management demands sensitivity and readiness on the part of managers, employers, parents and husbands to develop gender neutral attitudes.

The analysis and explanation of factors of gender inequality at the place of work has always been tended to feminist theorization of gender in modern societies (Walby). Workplace of 2000 will have many diversities including gender imbalances in organizations. This realization in the recent years has brought about diversity in movement integrating, women, minorities, seniors, disabled and the like into the day-to-day working of organizations.

There is need for both micro levels and macro levels analysis of gender practices in organization. Micro level strategies are based on participant's or worker's cognition, aspiration, perception, satisfaction expectation whereas macro level are based on societal factors influencing career choices and work life as shown in Fig. 1.

FIGURE 1
WOMEN AND WORK — A HUMAN RESOURCE MANAGEMENT MODEL

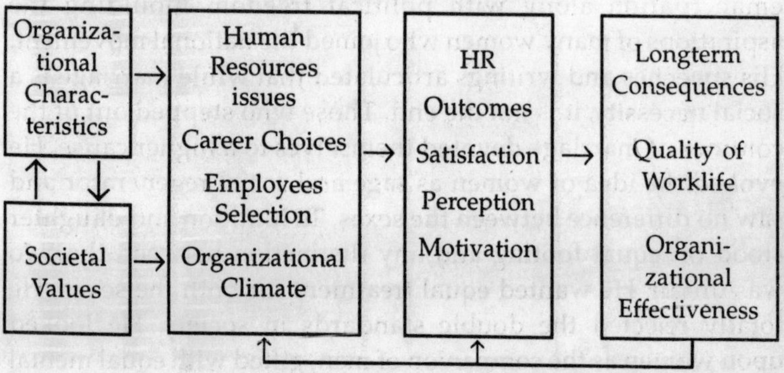

This book presents an analysis of various aspects of women in workforce. Human cognitions are the basis while presenting the theme. The chapters are organized in terms of historical organizational, psychological and developmental perspective of women and work with reference to Indian society, the entry of women as human resources, their career choices and development, their work perceptions, their quality of work life and the issues related to gender and work. The book finally suggests that one of the major factors changing the world of work today and in the next few years is the presence of women in every sphere of the organizational life. The managerial paradigms need to change in terms of perception and values and the organizations need management of changed strategies in the years to come.

Human Resource Management and Gender

Gender studies have become an important aspect of human resource management (HRM). In the recent years some of the major challenges of HRM are the issues of career choices, work designs, motivation and human resource development. It has been realized that without a committed workforce there cannot be any national development. Gender plays role in beliefs and ideology, arrangement of activities, meanings and experiences, diversity and changes at the place of work. Women constitute about fifty per cent of national population and are important as human resources.

The concern for development of women and their work life is not new to India. Gandhiji worked for the Indian women's emancipation along with political freedom moulding the aspirations of many women who joined the national movement. His speeches and writings articulated that while marriage is a social necessity, it is not the end. Those who stepped out of the confines of marriage devoted themselves to a higher cause. He evoked the idea of women as sage and social regenerator and saw no difference between the sexes. To him, son and daughter stood on equal footing and any distinction between the two was unfair. He wanted equal treatment for both the sexes. He totally rejected the double standards in society. He looked upon women as the companion of men, gifted with equal mental capacities and right to participate in the activities of man. His call to women to step out of the confines of their homes, to join the *prabhat pheries, satyagrahas* and other related activities that had grown as vehicles of political freedom, was out of the first attempt to draw Indian women out of the restricted circle of family life. His vision of freedom and equality of women heralded the inception of a movement in the early decade of the twentieth century. It also found expression in the formation of national bodies like the All India Women's Conferences (founded in 1920). The Women's Council (founded in 1920), the state level bodies like the Jyoti Sangha (1934) and in Gujarat and the Hindu Women's Rescue Home Society (1927). The decades between 1917 and 1947 witnessed the emergence of a number of women's organizations in the country. Their involvement in the strategies for political freedom had taken women a long way from the position they had reached as a result of women reformers themselves assuming leadership for their cause, and thus generated women's movements. They had made a bid for equality with men.

In the Indian Constitution there is mention of women's status in the following way "the State shall not discriminate against any citizen on grounds only of religion, race, caste, sex, place of birth or any of them (Right to equality), etc." Further it is mentioned that, "There shall be equality of opportunity for all citizens in matters relating to employment or appointment to any office under the State". The Constitution of independent India also granted franchise to women. The introduction of adult franchise along with the removal of all sorts of discrimination on sex, religion, caste or creed paved a way for further emancipation of women.

In the last decade of the present century, continuous increase of women in the work market has been observed all over the world. In India according to 1991 census, there were 91.39 million female workers as against the female population of 402 million. Women's work is not only a means of effective economy and raising the standard of living of the people, it has an equally important psychological perspective as women derive a sense of satisfaction in being considered valued members of the society. Since position in society and role in the community is largely dependent on work, it is seen as the means to satisfy human beings' need for belonging to a group and for a meaningful relation to others (Drucjer, 1877). The purpose of organization management and the essence of management philosophy is to make human strength productive. The system model of the performance of an individual highlights the two aspects of work behaviour for productivity. These are abilities and psychological arousals which include motivation, interests, dedication and commitment. Thus making commitment of women as an important area of study for productivity. Rantalaiho and Heiskanen (1997) while describing the concept of gender system, emphasize that a system should have an overall logic and all its element bound by set of rules, while considering gender systems as social and cultural source. Some of the issues about the women and work are perception, career choices, the role of relationship, autonomy and control, societal stereotypes, roles and socialization and the relationship between work and home life and designs of jobs.

Human resources refer to people in work organization having various abilities, talents and attitudes that influence productivity, quality and profitability. Individual's become human resources by virtue of the roles they assume in the work organizations. Work roles are defined and described so as to maximize particular employees contribution to achieve organizational goals.

Human beings are creative and complex resources whose behaviour is influenced by factors arising from the individual or his surrounding environment. Thus, organizational behaviour theorists suggest that behaviour and performance of human resource is a function of at least four variables: ability; motivation; role perception; and situational contingencies (McShare, 1992). Figure 2 presents similar ideas. On the other hand management is also viewed as facing two interrelated problems with regard to employees. These are the dual problems of 'control' and 'commitment' (Wats, 1986). Besides having varying level of abilities, aptitudes, skills and knowledge, personality, trait, gender, role perception and differences in experience, human resources also differ in motivation and commitment.

FIGURE 2

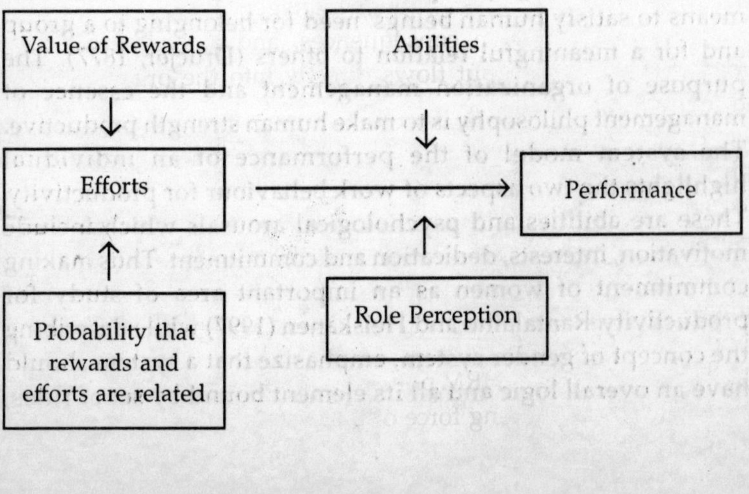

Human resource management deals with different approaches to the management of people in work organization. It is proactive and has a tendency to shift to an informal individualistic orientation (Storey, 1989, 1992).

The thrust of human resource management lies in delineating specific ways, based on organizational behaviour theory for achieving high performance. Abemathy (1983) expresses that building a truly competitive organization requires best efforts of workers. Their skills, commitment and enthusiasm are the means by which strategic goals get translated into practice.

There are a number of perspective to HRM. According to one perspective, HRM emphasizes the importance of high motivation, high commitment, communication and enlightened leadership. Most normative models of HRM, stress that human resources are assets rather than a cost and emphasize the commitment of employees as a source of competitive advantages (Legge, 1989). Understanding and having the best of human potential is based on organizational behaviour theories proposed by Maslow (1954) and Herzvberg (1966) and McGregor's theory Y (1960) suggesting how commitment and performance can be enhanced by leadership style. Another version of HRM emphasizes on the calculative, quantitative and strategic management aspects of managing the workforce in a rational way (Storey, 1989).

The analytical framework of the 'Harvard Model' by Beer et. al. (1984) consists of six basic components, which are, situational factors; stake holder interests; human management policy choices; HR outcomes; long-term consequences, and a feedback loop through, which the output flows directly into the organization and to the stake holders.

The model suggests that, the human resource outcomes are high when employees have commitment to organizational goals and high individual performance leading to cost effective products or services.

Guest (1989) has developed an alternative theoretical framework to show how HRM is different from orthodox personal management. This model has four main components: a set of HRM outcomes; a set of HRM policies; a number of organizational outcomes; and the binding force of the system.

POLICIES AND OUTCOMES OF HRM

HRM Policies	*HRM Outcomes*	*Organizational Outcomes*
Organization/job design		High job performance
Management of change	Strategic integration	High problem-solving change innovation
Recruitment, selection, socialization	Commitment	
Appraisal, training	Flexibility/adaptability	High cost-effectiveness
Development		
Reward system communication	Quality	Low turnover absence grievances
	Leadership/cultures/strategy	

Human Asset Accounting and Women

Management is often defined as controlling, planning, directing and motivating. Here the emphasis is only on motivating. This is not overlooking the importance of other aspects of management, but an attempt to put forward an indepth understanding of employee's performance in motivational perspective.

Therefore, the interface with other management strategies like planning, technical appraisals, time budgeting, financial budgeting, operations research and industrial relations are not the central concern here. The focal point here is the human asset accounting. Human asset or resource accounting are slowly beginning to have an effect. This concept formally recognizes the monetary value of a human being in an organization. If a good employee leaves the organization, the organization is at a loss not only because of the replacement cost but because of his individual worth. Likert (1967) suggests that level of intelligence, aptitude, quality of decision making, communication and control are some of the important variables in this context. Behavioural-oriented approach to employee's performance suggested in this study is thus important in human asset accounting and for preparing the organization for competitive advantage.

The review of HRM models suggests that some similarities

exist between the normative models of HRM and those of personal management. However, there are qualitative differences too. HRM assumes a unitary frame of reference; thus there will be no place in a company's HR strategy for those who threaten the continuity of the organization by attaching its basic aim (Bramham, 1989). The order of difference is that HRM, in theory is integrated into strategic planning. HRM also gives importance to cultural leadership. The purpose of cultural orientation is to provide employees with a commitment to certain beliefs and values. In HRM, stress is placed on the line managers responsibility of coordinating and directing all resources to generate commitment and enthuse subordinates to innovate. Nevertheless, HRM in theory emphasizes, the importance of individual, human growth and developing the management 'team'.

The concept of HRM which started in 1970's, replacing and modifying the boundaries of personal management has undergone yet another development in the recent years. This is adding the concept of strategy to management. Moving from the earlier maintenance-based approach, development aspects dominate the HRM systems today. Strategic management attempts to integrate the situational factors and suggestions that flexibility in managing is important. Some of the factors being considered in the strategic human resource management are turbulence, leading the organization to recognize the importance of human resources in performance of organization, the cognitive and therefore human nature of strategy process, the managerial paradigms, the management of change, the organization dynamics and need to attend and implement human dimension, which pervades these processes. In this context also gender becomes an important aspect, particularly in a country like India, where there is an extremely fast pace of technological and social development and there is turbulence all over in terms of human expectations and aspirations. This book emphasizes on gender and working, as this appears as one of the most significant issues of strategic HRM today. However, the definition of strategy as per dictionary (directing military movements) seems to be changing with business organizations now. Applied to working and organizations the strategic elements may be categorized into three main areas:

1. The strategic process,
2. The leadership, and
3. Organization effectiveness.

The strategic process includes deploying human resource contribution as an asset and hence, resource is an important aspect of the process of strategically managed human resource and is the key to successful business today. The recent realization and an addition to management thinking thus is accepting the diversity at the place of work. In this book we are discussing one major factor — the gender issue.

The next chapter takes a look at the historical and social theorizing and development related to 'work, gender and organization'.

TWO

Work, Gender and Organizations

Schools of Thoughts

Work, gender and organization relationships have evolved and theorized by different schools of thought in different ways. Yet there appears a thread of commonality in these explanations. Experience is considered as the most important aspect of gender. The liberal feminist theory was evolved during, the seventeenth and eighteenth century during the time when industrialization was starting. Women's status was that of non-persons under the funded systems. They had no voting or property rights. The concept of equality evolved as a result of realization that women cannot find full satisfaction of the life exclusively in their roles as wife and mother, and a rational and just society allowed fulfilment of every individual through a system of individual rights. The emphasis in this theory is on incompletely as a result of system of male domination which is the fundamental principal of patriarchal society.

The 1960's liberal movement (Deckand, 1979) rose out of dissatisfaction of women with sexism. It aimed at a new social order where women are not subordinate to men and proposed alternative social, economic, political and cultural values challenging male dominated culture. Emphasizing on the positive side of the qualities of women, i.e., as a nurturer, expressiveness and sensitivity to the concept of women was underlined. Kones (1989) suggests participation in decision making and leadership, flexible design of jobs, equitable distribution of income and political accountability as the elements to facilitate feminist practices in organizations. Under this approach experiences and lives of women became the source of theorizing and basic organizational concepts like career, work and management were redefined.

Freudian and psycho-analytic theories looked at the difference in feminist roles because of specific social arrangements affecting psychological development. For example, the structure of patriarchal family results into general gender development and subordination of women to men. In a healthy society there should be no gender structuring. It is also expected that in today's society since both the parents are working they share equal responsibility of children's upbringing.

Marxist feminist theory, however, considered gender as structural and materialistic, similar to class characterized domination and approach. As a synthesis of Marxist, psychologist and radical feminism, Jaggan (1983) emerged with the socialist feminist theory. Gender, according to this approach, is considered a result of social relationship based on perceived differences. It is believed that organization, families and societies can be understood as separate sections as they constitute gender relations.

Post modern feminist theories emphasize on social reality and subjectivity. Women's experience and standpoint provide an important strategy for organizational discourse. The Third World post colonial theorizing considers the constitution of complex subjectivity beyond Western conception of sex/gender focusing on gendered aspects of globalization processes (Prakash, 1995).

As the ideas in the work-related feminist theories were developing all over the world, in India too there was great concern about the issue. Vivekananda called this as Shakti-worshipper—one who knows that God is an omnipresent force and sees in women the manifestation of that force implying that women are great forces and could be prime movers of society. Gender looked upon women as the companion of men and gifted with equal mental capacities. India's Constitution also says that "there shall be equality of employment for all citizens" and "The State shall not discriminate against any citizen on grounds only of religion, race, caste, sex, place of birth or any of them."

Today Indian organizations are gearing up to face the new challenges of workforce diversity. Social change has brought about greater aspiration and expectation among women and their perception of lives have changed. They, no more, view life only in terms of family and children. Their world view has changed and career work life and organizational life give them greater confidence, autonomy, inner development and social prestige.

Only a decade ago the idea that women had a basic right to work, was radical. However since then, we have seen attitudes of Indians changing drastically. Now more women are employed and more men have accepted this happily. Today, well-educated women no longer have much of an option about work. For such women values have reversed. It is not only assumed that they are employed, but considered almost abnormal if they are not. In a survey of girls studying in Indian Institute of Technology, Delhi it was found that 100 per cent girls were looking forward to challenging careers.

There appear two interrelated changes in attitudes about work. People increasingly feel that work provides or should provide the opportunity for self-fulfilment. More than any other way, work is perceived as the way to creativity, responsibility and through work, self-actualization can be achieved. Women are actively seeking work in order to develop their own potentials. Working in organization is a way of life today.

In USA between, 1947 to 1975 female population increased by 32 per cent and female workforce by 123 per cent, the labour force being defined as everyone aged, 16 or above, who is employed and seeking employment. The largest increase has been in the number of working mothers and wives. In 1970, in families where husbands were present, one-fourth of mothers of children less than one to three years were employed. In India too there is a significant increase in the technical women force.

When half of a population does something, then behaviour is not deviant but considered normal. Until 1970s it may have been normal for women to have a job but not a career and it was acceptable only if there were no small children at home or income was a necessity. With constrained job opportunities and limiting conditions, most women who worked in the earlier days, the majority were married with children and they did it in order to improve economic status of their family. Work for women was thus an extension of their traditional role as labour forces. As long as women do jobs and not careers they derive their status from their husband's identity. They being wage earners and mothers, think their husband's job important and they feel guilty or worried about effect of their job on family if they work for a career. Even today their work is based on traditional values and there hasn't been much change even though today number of women want to work in order to develop their potentials and they insist that to work is their right. This is a change in traditional values in India in this decade.

This has resulted in overall development of women. As they get an opportunity to earn success, knowledge and ambition, they develop competence and assume leadership as men have. They are realizing that they also, like men, are individuals. Women's commitment to career reflect their desire to fulfil their own potentials. It is a specific objective of derived status of identity based on being in a relationship.

Work therefore, is supposed to provide fulfilment and creativity but never drudgery or sweat. This modern view is in contrast with earlier views, which essentially defined work as what one has to do even unpleasantly. Women are also choosing work because at times they are looking for egocentric gratification.

A good percentage of all working women want influential careers. To attain this requires new lifestyles with clear gains and costs of which are sometimes predictable and sometimes unknown. While payoffs are greater, careers are enormously more costly in terms of commitment than jobs.

Sexism in Employment

Fifty per cent of the world population comprise women and they form nearly half the workforce. Therefore it is highly logical to consider their work life, working conditions, psychology, problems and measures to optimize their productivity and satisfaction.

A variety of myths support the sex typing of occupation and other discriminatory practices that have hampered many working women in pursuing their goals. However, while myths die hard and social practices change slowly, progress is still occurring. With much ado, the problem has to be approached with a positive frame of mind and make women comfortable in their jobs.

Organizational employment frequently practices sexism. For

instance the assumption that only someone with a single-minded commitment, ambition and achievement is worth hiring, is often accompanied by the presumption that such an attitude is characteristic of men (never of women). This is also evident in the denial that responsibility of child-care and household logistics has anything to do with management and policy decisions. Women also experience discrimination at the place of work in terms of promotions and recognition, formally and attitudes and actions informally. It is also manifested in preference of men to work with men and earn respect and rewards from men.

Organizational sexism is based on the fact that most of the decision makers are men. Men are reared with the initial idea that they are different from and implicitly better than women. Since there are so few outstanding successful women, most men do not want women who are their successful peers and their superiors. Few men realize that competence is asexual, and hence their preconceived notions are rarely challenged.

Women are least accepted where work involves being independent and innovative, assuming leadership and having power. The expectation that women lack such qualities and skills is perhaps the most potent and injurious form of sexism because the basic assumption at work is 'masculine' qualities are best.

Because of stereotypic views of work situation we set on what behaviour is appropriate. Keeping women out of positions of responsibility and power is based on the rejection of personality characteristics women are supposed to have. When their qualities are perceived like those of the men they are judged as manly (negative). If they have feminine qualities they are seen as incompetent. Such attitudes have harmed working women immensely.

Even though in the last several years, emphasis in management has changed to include new sensitivity to handling peoples as well as profits. Sexist bias still remains in the corporate world. Much of what managers do, obviously involves, motivating, manipulating and encouraging people. Organizations pay more attention to women to learn to be assertive to develop qualities considered masculine. But sexism makes women's need to change, more visible, and seemingly more inappropriate than that of men.

In spite of new liberal values, most men and women still think of intellectual, independent and ambitious people as masculine and supportive and interdependent as feminine. A competitive situation requires willingness to compete, seriousness of purpose, willingness to give up affection for possibility of control and power and a need to assert oneself. People are more comfortable when women do not show these characteristics overtly, nor display their enjoyment of power so clearly.

In a survey carried out among the various work groups it was found that groups with higher proportion of women were more passive and restrained, but as expected they give higher productivity.

Working women who are married and have children, have generally not pursued a career with success in the same single-mindedness as men. But is this the cost of success. Women must now learn to compete and use power and succeed within the establishments. So far only a few women are in positions of significant power, and their objectives and styles do not seem to be much different from those of men.

THREE

Women and Work: The Indian Scenario

It is being realized in the recent years that women are important participants in the development process. However, there has always been a discrepancy between the idealized notions of the status of women and the real life perceptions of women themselves all over the world. Indian scenario has been different than the other countries in terms of rigid hierarchical structures in which women were denied opportunities of intellectual pursuits, education and creativity. As a result of the joint effect of neglect of education, customs and attitudes degradation in the status of women in India became evident.

The role of women in Indian society has been changing over the centuries. The male-female complementary concept of the Vedic India gave way to the notion of a male supremacy in the subsequent period of Indian history. Indian women too with social changes and development, developed confidence to appraise their positions in society and occupy prominent places in the social structure. However, this was partly under the influence of western culture and education that Indian women have been taking up the challenges for equal recognition and opportunities, consciously or unconsciously. Today, as a result of these factors, women constitute a significant part of technically trained personnel in India.

Indian society has witnessed tremendous socio-cultural changes in the recent years. These are particularly evident in infrastructure, spread of education, emancipation of women, awareness of political rights and associated consciousness of rights and privileges.

Every developing nation would believe that education is the

heart of developmental process. Since women are considered to be prime movers of the society, their education should assume great relevance for the progress and development of society. During the last few decades of this century, however, women in Indian society have been gaining recognition and support. As a result, women are entering into a variety of occupations, like medicines, education, media, engineering, architecture and management. There has been a noticeable change in our country in the attitude of men towards women in recent years, which is a positive factor for women's development.

Today women dominate the field of nursing and are in good numbers in medicine, computer science, research and education. Women are entering in other fields of science and technology based professions and are occupying high positions. In the field of science and technology, although there is a vast scope for women's employment, suitable women candidates aren't found in adequate numbers in architecture, engineering and similar fields, because women tend to choose professions that are culturally an extension of their role as housewives and which allow them to reconcile with their family life. On the other hand society also expects the same stereotyped role of women, though with a difference. Section studies attempt to highlight some factors related to gender as a variable in human resource management. Participation of women in science and technology is not only an important aspect in the social and economic development of the nation, it is a critical constituent in the process of improving the quality of life of women themselves. All over the world, but more so in the developing world, the low participation of women in science and technology courses has been a matter of concern and the need for improvement of the situation is beyond doubt.

Many studies have shown that women are more committed to their work, compared to their male counterparts.

Parikh and Sukhatme (1992) in their detailed study on the participation of women in engineering courses and profession reported that percentage of women taking up engineering courses is increasing. Data on job status revealed that 66.3 per cent were employed, 2.4 per cent were self-employed and the rest were postgraduate students. Their salaries, however, were low and their pace of career development was slow.

Barriers at Work

Almost all the studies in America and some of the studies by Indian scholars indicate that there is overt and subtle gender discrimination. The findings on the hidden processes of gender discrimination of women physicians in the US are probably common to the experience of women physicians in other countries as well and many of these processes have been found in other professions also.

The studies report that an adequate explanation of the under representation of women physicians at the top levels of the medical profession is not only because of their modest ambition, low prestige, specialities, their relegation to family responsibilities but much more due to the sorting and sifting process of sponsorship and patronage, the help and hinderance of colleagues and husbands. These factors explain women physicians' success or lack of it.

Some of the male gatekeepers do not yet believe that women have the capability to work as their men colleagues. The tendency is to offer opportunities of advancement to those similar to their own background. Women also seem to be unfamiliar with the game of self-presentation. They are not able to negotiate for important positions in the organization and thus their worth gets ignored by their male colleagues and men in the larger professional network. Studies also suggest that women have to be better than men to attain the same status (Pugh and Waterman, 1983, Piliavin, 1976, Olson and Miller, 1989) in organizations.

During recommendation of position, promotion, officership in professional associations, etc., competence is often evaluated only in professional discussions. As most of the women are soft spoken they are likely to be overlooked. In the male dominated work world, there is an aggressive self-advancement desire in women. Successful careers in medicine are built through combination of sponsorship, visibility and reciprocal favours. The career analysis of the physicians interviewed by Lober (1984) show that professional development is as dependent on the action of colleagues and superiors as on the person concerned. Annapurni (1986) and Kalarani (1987), report that Indian women follow a policy of avoiding unpleasant situations to avoid discrimination and harassment and hence do not go up the ladder in careers. Sex segregation leads to interaction with colleagues of the same sex and often women physicians also become more dependent on their physician husbands for pursuing their careers.

Constraints at Home and Work Life

Indian society is tradition bound with a male dominated society and cherishes different values. Marriage is very important in the lives of Indian women and social attitudes do not favour women remaining single. Parents consider arranging the marriage of their daughters as their responsibility, even when they are mature adult professionals. This has brought more complexities particularly when community factors have to be considered. Today women professionals are in great demand due to their potential for earning as well as the prestige of the profession. Most of the women physicians marry men from the same profession or at least with equal professional status (Annapurni, 1986).

Women physicians consider family as their prime responsibility and managing of home is done with the help from family members or hired help. Strong supportive family network is a positive factor in Indian setting enabling women professionals to combine work and career.

The question of husbands sharing domestic responsibilities or child care does not arise, as both physician husbands and wives consider men helping in these responsibilities as untraditional Kalarani (1987) and Sinha (1987). They also state that women professionals do feel guilty of neglecting their children and they regret that they do not have even time to spend with them. But the women physicians in government/quasi-government service are entitled to three-month maternity leave, medical leave and leave without pay, etc. Hence they are able to combine their career with domestic and child care without career interruptions.

American studies also report that marriage brings with it problems of not having enough time for spouse, and critical issues of the dual career. The dual burden has affected women physicians all the time and continues to shape their career choices. This is reflected in the social world of men and women all over the globe.

In the US, only two-thirds of women physicians were married in contrast to national average of 90 per cent of female non-physicians. Only 60-70 per cent of the married women physicians had children in contrast to 90 per cent of the male physicians having children. Women physicians had fewer children and were older when they had their children (Martin and Arnold, 1987).

A 1982 study reported that 75 per cent of the women physicians surveyed stated that they were personally responsible for most housework in their homes. Another study found that 50 per cent of male physicians agreed with the statement that women physicians, who spend long hours at work, neglected their responsibilities towards their family. Between 30 to 60 per cent women physicians felt that family and career conflicts were important influences on their lives. Another study found that women explicitly sought regular and shorter working hours because of concerns regarding family life.

A plausible interpretation of all these data could be that women choose lower prestige specialization, shorter working hours, etc., as they are more amenable to integrating their personal and professional lives with non-traditional ideas about family life. Women have also reported more social isolation from same sex peers than men. Women wished to have a spouse who had a higher degree of career commitment, hence the trend has been that women planned either to be single and remain employed full time or married have children and choose to remain employed part time or in jobs like school teaching, typist, etc.

Situational Barriers and Work Life

Roby (1972) has identified a number of situational barriers. The most pervasive barrier is sex discrimination in general. Freeman (1975) reported that there was less encouragement for female students than for their male counterpart. It is also observed that there is a general climate of male preferences especially in male dominated settings (Bourne and Weaklier, 1982). In the engineering college itself, women experience sex discrimination. 78.6 per cent of the students experience sex discrimination from the male students, 37 per cent from laboratory partners, 30 per cent from male laboratory instructors, and 44 per cent from male faculty according to a study by Horst (1981). 65 per cent of the women interviewed in the study perceived sex discrimination in the field of engineering. A widely shared perception is that sex discrimination in engineering is more than in the other fields. A substantial significant proportion of women reported sexual harassment from both faculty and students. Sexual harassment included unwanted comments, sexual suggestions, sexual advances, which puts one in an uncomfortable position.

Indian women engineers have not reported any major sexual harassment. But some have reported subtle sexual discrimination. Chaturvedi (1985) states that the women engineers had sexual discrimination more from the bosses of their own sex than from male bosses. Women bosses were more strict and authoritative than the men bosses, and are understanding and considerate. Women engineers in India faced difficulties working outdoors, supervising construction work, specially in villages. They faced conveyance difficulties. This is more due to socio-cultural reasons. They could not use two wheelers wearing a 'sari' and villagers did not approve of their wearing pants. They could not travel at late hours because travelling with men colleagues was not approved by family members. Women engineers also found it difficult to extract work from male subordinates, Lober (1984) and manage the contractors. Very few women took part in activities connected with the professional associations. Venkatratnam (1971) reported that groups not taking part in the activities of professionals was one of the reasons for their not climbing the social and professional ladder.

With a demanding job, full of competition, women engineers face professional role expectations which are not congruent with feminine role expectations. Marriage is important in the lives of most of the Indian women. It is also true that women professionals are in great demand in the marriage market today due to their potentials and prestige. Most of the women engineers in India tend to get married to men from the same profession or persons with equal professional status. Arranged marriages and dowry practices are common even now, although there are less dowry expectations from women engineers and professionals.

The status of Indian women has undergone a gradual change. The privileged position of women in the Vedic period has also changed completely. Professional women are no more in bonds or sole begetters of children and housekeepers. They do not look down upon themselves and submit to the authority/superiority of the men.

Unfortunately, the leaders of our society have not realized that participation of women in economic, social and political life will be an impetus for progress. They have also failed to tap the potentials of human resources of half the population of our country. Even to this date emancipation of women is not complete. The glorification of practices like dowry and any other deplorable social evil affects not only women but the overall progress of the nation.

Why Women take up Employment

Do women really want to contribute as human resources? In this section an analysis of why women work is presented. According to labour bureau report, the basic factors are motivational forces for women's employment, particularly for employment of mothers. These are:

(i) Permanent and growing inadequacy in the overall income of the family,
(ii) Temporary fall in family's income due to exceptional or accidental circumstances such as the sickness, etc.,
(iii) The death of the breadwinner,
(iv) Woman's desire for economic independence, and
(v) Need and perception of 'women's liberation' equality, etc., advocated by some women in west India. This type is, however smaller in number in India.

These reasons are mainly economical and they do not account for other motivational reasons. In some cases women may take up employment to evaluate their talent, or interest. Others work to utilize their free time or education or they work for personal satisfaction. There is yet another group of professional women who may be working to gain recognition and importance. In a comparative study of 57 men and 90 women interesting results have emerged. These are discussed later.

Why men object to women taking up jobs cannot be explained in one word, yet it appears that reasons are embedded in the attitude they hold. Traditionally they feel the 'Lakshmi' of the house should remain at home. Often a stigma is attached to women's employment, because sometimes it might hurt the male ego. This might be perceived as neglect of the family, household and especially the children. There is also a fear that a working woman tends to develop a tendency to overrule her husband.

Problem Faced by Working Women

The perception of people change when a woman takes up a career.

Another difficult problem is her ambivalence and sense of guilt. Not only does she try to work hard, but she also tries to prove herself as a good mother and a wife. Moreover, often family provides little help to rationalize her role.

This state of affairs though serious is not unexpected. Women have started to break away from male subjugation and are taking up jobs to shape their own personalities. However small the percentage of women moving out of the protective environment of their homes to seek work and employment, their numbers are fast increasing and are likely to constitute a significant portion of the workforce in the next decade. However, there are different perceptions about females and males (Tables 3.1 and 3.2).

TABLE - 3.1

PERCEPTION OF FEMALE TRAITS AND ROLES

Perception	*Female Role Playing*
Soft spoken	Good communication
Interested in own appearance	Tactful communicators
Believes in luck/God	
Orderly habits	Gentle
Not competitive	
Need for security	Quite
Introvert	
Interest in art and literature	Religious/God fearing
Emotional	
Expresses tender feelings	Aware of feelings of others
Caring	

TABLE - 3.2
PERCEPTION OF MALE TRAITS

Perception		*Male Role Play*
Aggressive	May use harsh words	Feelings not easily hurt
Independent	Security is not the concern	Adventurous
Less emotional	Impulsive	Makes decisions easily
Emotions not expressed		Never cries
Objective	Extrovert	Acts as a leader
Not easily influenced		Self-confident
Dominant	High male chauvinism	Ambitious
Likes maths and science		Independent
Not excitable	Believes in hard work	Not concerned about appearance
Active		
Competitive		Thinks men are superior to women
Logical		Uses strategies and facts
Worldly		Knows s of the world
Skilled in business		

Our culture has assigned different roles to men and women. These roles move around women's child bearing functions and men's characteristics and their qualifications. In a survey of 57 men and 90 women, 13.3 per cent women and 15.8 per cent men feel that circumstances forced them to take up this job. Only 15.6 per cent women and 12.3 per cent men have taken up this job because it is highly satisfying. Social influence is seen only in case of 4.4 per cent women not in men. Similarly "job is the 'in' thing" has been rated lease - none of the men and only 1.1 per cent women have given this choice. Coming to financial soundness of the job, 8.8 per cent men and 3.3 per cent women have taken up the present job for this reason. Growth potential of the job has been recognized by 3.3 per cent women and 5.3 per cent men. Status/identity seems important for 8.8 per cent men and 5.6 per cent women. Job as productive utilization of time is seen in 2.2 per cent women and also 3.5 per cent in men. Maximum number of those employed are in the pay scale of Rs five thousand to eight thousand. For men in this salary group the most important reason is job suited to the qualifications, whereas for women in addition to this, circumstances forcing them is an important reason. It is interesting to note that there are only 2.2 per cent and 1.1 per cent women in the salary group of 17,000-20,000 and 20,000 and above. Tables 3.3 and 3.4 present these results.

Apart from expecting each sex to perform different tasks, our culture expects men and women to differ also in their psychological characteristics. These sex roles are results of cultural beliefs and expectations about the different behaviours and characteristics that people think should be associated with members of each sex. The traits dominant in the roles prescribed for females primarily relate to and facilitate social concerns and interpersonal warmth. For males on the other hand the traits are basically related to personal competence and achievement (Table 3.4). Women are expected to be gentle, sensitive to other's feelings, and emotional dependent and ambitious. Furthermore not only are members of each expected to display "appropriate traits", but they are also expected not to have traits considered definitive of the other sex. Thus, roles demand mutual exclusiveness in relevant psychological traits. It is a high degree of achievement motivation that is also one of the prime motivations for women to work. They do not consider themselves to be inferior to males in any way. Though they constitute the minority of the women workforce they are the most visible and dominant of all the classes of women.

Problems of Working Women

Invariably, working women face some problems, which are common to all classes. At the family level, women are expected to do their routine domestic chores, along with their jobs. Even the educated and professionally qualified women in India often find it difficult to escape the disadvantages of womanhood at the place of work. Their dual responsibilities—as earners and as housewives—leave them with no free time for thought and action that their male counterparts enjoy in the Indian society. Women have to work harder to keep a balance among organizational commitment, job commitment, interpersonal commitment and family commitment.

TABLE 3.3
WHY WOMEN WORK

Table shows percentage of women for different reasons for taking of jobs in different salary groups

Total Family Income (in Rs.)	*1*	*2*	*3*	*4*	*5*	*6*	*7*	*8*	*9*	*10*	*X*	
1,000- 5,000	2.2	3.3	2.2	1.1	-	1.1	-	2.2	1.1	-	-	(13.3)
5,000- 8,000	10	6.7	3.3	1.1	-	1.1	2.2	3.3	0	1.1	-	(28.9)
8,000-11,000	8.9	1.1	4.4	2.2	1.1	1.1	1.1	-	1.1	-	-	(21.1)
11,000-14,000	13.3	1.1	2.2	-	-	-	-	-	2.2	1.1	-	(20)
14,000-17,000	7.8	1.1	2.2	-	-	-	-	-	1.1	-	1	(13.3)
17,000-20,000	1.1	-	1.1	-	-	-	-	-	-	-	-	(2.2)
Above 20,000	1.1	-	-	-	-	-	-	-	-	-	-	(1.1)
X	-	-	-	-	-	-	-	-	-	-	-	(0)
	44.4	13.3	15.6	4.4	1.1	3.3	3.3	5.6	5.6	2.2	1.1	(100)

The respondents are from different income groups:

1. Job suited to my qualifications
2. Circumstances forced to take up job
3. For job satisfaction
4. Friend's/Social influence
5. Doing job is in fashion
6. For becoming financially sound
7. Job has promotional avenues
8. It gives identity/social status
9. Utilization of time in productive way
10. Any other reason

TABLE 3.4
WHY MEN WORK

Table shows percentage of men for different reasons for taking of jobs in different salary groups

Total Family Income (in Rs.)	1	2	3	4	5	6	7	8	9	10	X	
1,000- 5,000	7	3.5	-	0	0	-	-	-	-	1.8	-	(12.3)
5,000- 8,000	12.3	1.8	3.5	0	-	-	3.5	8	1.8	-	-	(29.8)
8,000-11,000	5.3	8.8	1.8	0	-	5.3	-	1.8	1.8	-	-	(24.6)
11,000-14,000	8.8	-	3.5	0	-	-	-	-	-	-	-	(12.3)
14,000-17,000	5.3	-	-	0	-	1.8	1.8	-	-	1.8	-	(10.5)
17,000-20,000	0	-	-	0	-	-	-	-	-	-	-	0
Above 20,000	0	1.8	3.5	0	-	1.8	-	-	1.8	-	-	(8.8)
X	1.8	-	-	0	-	-	-	-	-	-	-	(1.8)
	40.4	15.8	12.3	0	0	8.8	5.3	8.8	5.3	3.5	0	(100)

The respondents are from different income groups:

1. Job suited to my qualifications
2. Circumstances forced to take up job
3. For job satisfaction
4. Friend's/Social influence
5. Doing job is in fashion
6. For becoming financially sound
7. Job has promotional avenues
8. It gives identity/social status
9. Utilization of time in productive way
10. Any other reason

The role of women has received attention and close examination only in the last two decades. After the declaration of International Year of Women in 1975, attention was focused on the problems of women all over the world. Sharma (1989) states that the women's movement, as it currently unfolds itself beyond its traditional concerns with legislation, education and political participation, with multiplicity of forms, diversity of concern and motivation and ideological orientation, brings together several perspectives and raises several issues in terms of status of women. She quotes from the Third National Conference on Women's Studies 1986, that the women's question and implication of the principle of gender equality adopted in the Fundamental Rights Resolution represents one of these unresolved debates.

Report of the Fourth World Conference on Women at Beijing 1995 states that making women equal partners in the national development processes and equipping them to make choices in order to actualize their self-worth through empowerment are goals to which the government is committed.

In India from the Fifth Five Year Plan (1974-79) onwards there has been a shift in the approach from welfare to development of women. The Eighth Five Year Plan (1992-97), promises to ensure that the benefits of development from different sectors do not bypass women. The flow of benefits to women in the three core sectors of education, health and employment are to be vigilantly monitored. Women must be enabled to function as equal partners and participants in the development process. As part of this effort many policy instruments have been brought forth over the years. One of the significant documents which emerged from the International Decade for Women was the Forward Looking Strategies for the Advancement of Women (FLS). In this document the relationship among the three goals of equality development and peace was stressed along with full participation and integration of women in all areas of society (NPPW, 1988).

While presenting an overview of urban work participation rate of women (Saxena, 1991) delineated a sharp rise in the number of urban women workers in India during the period 1971-81, i.e. 14.22 per cent in 1971 to 19.67 per cent in 1981. During this period, the growth rate of urban women workers has been higher than that of urban women population. In majority of the urban women prone industries and occupations, the intensity of women proneness increased. Certain occupations like nursing, health visitors and teachers continue to be largely dominated by urban women workers.

The female work participation rate rose to 22.27 in 1991 (Registrar General and Census Commissioner, India, New Delhi). This shows that women contribute greatly to the economy. Employment of women is an index of their economic status in society, specially with reference to their equality. Ghosh (1991) focused on the Canadian education giving references of the countries, including India, emphasizing that education has a significant role to play in the rapid and radical change in the social profile because of the pressing social change and of work in an information age.

Banerjee (1995) expressed that in quantitative terms, education of women in India has achieved progress but this has not helped to change the attitudes and values of men or women in the direction of real equality. The discrepancy between the idealized concept of women and their real life situations has been recognized (Jaiswal, 1993). The social attitudes, rituals, authoritarian structure of the family and organizations are some of the detrimental factors for wastage of human resources. Women's participation in economic life is characterized by inequality and constraints in getting out of household chores and responsibility comes in their way of progress. Spuriock and Ribinwitz (1990) point out that although there are greater opportunities and options for women to pursue a carrier in western countries, barriers and inequalities continue, to play roles.

The changing status of women in the post independence era was studied by Hate (1969) touching various facets of women's life including their carrier employment and motherhood. The sample was drawn from educated middle-class working and non-working women. The author concluded that the status of women in India is in the process of change in the positive direction though very slow and incomplete. Nevertheless it is felt that work is critically important for women to experience a sense of identity. Baruch Barnett and Rivers (1985) believe that there is profound difference between the impact of paid work and home making.

The Kinds of Jobs Women Choose

As a result of aforesaid factors and developments there is notion of sex related job-types in our society. Certain jobs have been accepted by our society as feminine and women are encouraged to go towards these jobs. Women are mostly concentrated in occupations like school teaching, nursing, stenographers and typing, they also work as telephone-operators and are in medicine. Those who work in industrial occupations are generally in jobs which need delicate handling of the material. There are certain women who take up other jobs too but they are few and do not constitute a significant proportion of the women workforce. So far as types of industries are concerned women are seen working in garments, electronics and packaging in large numbers most often women are paid less, though it is more prevalent in unorganized occupations at lower levels. Even though it is not recognized, yet women workers are playing major roles in Indian agriculture and many unorganized sectors like brick making, bidi making, etc.

Women also face problems while dealing with co-workers since time immemorial they have been regarded as naturally inferior. They have to work harder to prove themselves to be "equal" to her co-workers. Being in a position lower than a woman on a job hurts man's self-esteem. For women, promotions are hard to come and words of praise are rare, some women might feel unnatural in an all men dominant work environment. But some interesting facts have emerged. Some professions like 'library science' are popular as a career choice for women. In fact they are a first preference. But for most men it may be the last preference. This creates a situation of mismatch. Women may be sophisticated and highly motivated and men most demotivated. This creates a work culture on ambivalence.

Several industries (banking, health care, etc.) have had a higher proportion of women in their workforce and they have been hiring many more. However, there are very few at the managerial levels. In skilled trades jobs (e.g., construction, steel and roads) women are rare indeed. With respect to white-collar jobs, women hold fifty per cent of all clerical positions, thirty per cent of all bank jobs and most of the bookkeeping jobs. As managers, women comprise only ten per cent at entry level, five per cent of middle level positions and less than one per cent reach top level jobs. However, women's work as doctors with medical degree has doubled since the last decade. Some interesting aspects based on the census of technical personnel are presented in the following Tables.

TABLE - 3.5
SECTORWISE EMPLOYMENT OF MALES AND FEMALES

Year 1981

Field	*Male*		*Female*	
	Pub.	*Pvt.*	*Pub.*	*Pvt.*
Agricultural Science	39404	4449	379	43
Science	211923	70165	27693	11316
Veterinary Science	11343	728	125	5
Engineering & Technology	227566	63298	3233	1415
Medicine — Allopathy	31863	4274	7411	1748
— Others	9301	1807	779	262
Nursing	488	101	4384	1361
Education	71535	34907	18560	14148
All combined	663452	203980	64660	31194

All combined includes fields 'not given', other and ITI's
Medicine other includes Unani, Dentistry, Homeopathy, Ayurvedic
Source: Degree Holders and Technical personnel Survey, Census 1951; Division for Scientific & Technical Personnel; Council of Scientific & Industrial Research, New Delhi.

TABLE - 3.6

DISTRIBUTION OF EMPLOYED DEGREE HOLDERS AND TECHNICAL PERSONNEL ACCORDING TO NATURE OF WORK, SECTOR OF EMPLOYMENT, QUALIFICATION AND SEX

		Male		*Female*	
Field	*Qualification*	*Pub.*	*Pvt.*	*Pub.*	*Pvt.*
Agricultural Science	Ph.D	1966	145	27	0
	P.G. Degree	9731	786	92	24
	Graduate	26344	3384	253	18
	Combined	39404	4449	379	43
Science	Ph.D	8501	1987	1035	294
	P.G. Degree	54265	19587	7579	4681
	Graduate	147573	48193	18889	6212
	Combined	211923	70165	27673	11316
Veterinary Science	P.G.Degree	1457	100	33	2
	Graduate	8440	546	81	3
	Combined	11343	728	125	5
Engineering & Technology	Ph.D	2011	523	39	3
	P.G. Degree	11283	4471	168	44
	P.G. Diploma	3190	1376	124	64
	Graduate	87696	27769	905	396
	Undergraduate	123141	29090	1994	907
	Combined	227566	63298	3233	1415
Medicine Allopathy	P.G. Degree	9284	1348	2023	417
	P.G. Diploma	3730	473	1253	271
	Graduate	17433	2186	3934	1013
	Combined	31863	4214	7411	1748
Education	P.G. Degree	16290	7926	3683	2594
	Graduate	54620	26632	14691	11490
	Combined	71535	34907	18560	14148
Combined	Combined	663452	203980	64668	31194

TABLE - 3.7
COMPARISON ACCORDING TO SALARY

Field	Salary Slab	Male		Female	
		Pub.	Pvt.	Pub.	Pvt.
Agricultural Science	I	11293	1318	137	15
	II	11871	826	111	1
	III	5884	451	62	1
	IV	2290	249	6	6
	V	175	117	0	6
	Combined	39404	4449	379	43
Science	I	82636	20097	13914	3496
	II	44092	13510	4777	1874
	III	24854	8642	1645	747
	IV	13617	4385	568	126
	V	2060	2161	91	54
	Combined	211923	70165	27673	11316
Veterinary Science	I	2328	81	51	1
	II	4650	236	42	1
	III	1944	83	13	1
	IV	392	104	1	0
	V	28	60	0	0
	Combined	11343	728	125	5
Engineering & Technology	I	61987	11184	1514	461
	II	64621	13202	707	151
	III	36266	8987	281	87
	IV	23149	9284	95	47
	V	3434	6286	29	32
	Combined	227566	63298	3233	1415
Medicine Allopathy	I	3254	678	727	431
	II	9002	898	2263	416
	III	8182	644	1766	185
	IV	4536	443	907	118
	V	709	235	69	37
	Combined	31863	4274	7411	1748
Education	I	42020	19372	11446	7842
	II	11728	4878	2252	1273
	III	2394	1017	365	146
	IV	425	127	71	12
	V	112	36	19	25
	Combined	71535	34907	18560	14148

(Contd.)

Field	*Salary Slab*	*Male*		*Female*	
		Pub.	*Pvt.*	*Pub.*	*Pvt.*
Combined	I	238287	62399	31629	13139
	II	156140	35954	11007	3884
	III	81371	20393	4275	1236
	IV	44903	14875	1691	320
	V	6708	8999	218	164
	Combined	663452	203980	64668	31194

Salary Slab:
I - 500 - 1000
II - 1000 - 1500
III - 1500 - 2000
IV - 2000 - 3000
V - 3000 & above (5)

TABLE - 3.8
THE DIFFERENT CONSTITUENTS OF S&T WOMEN PERSONNEL BY THEIR FIELDS OF SPECIALIZATION

Field	*Per cent*
Agriculture	3.6
Science	41.02
Veterinary Science	0.82
Engineering & Technology	24.6
Medicine Allopathy	5.48
Indigenous medicine	2.6
Dentistry	0.19
Nursing	0.48
I.I.T. certificate holder	11.03
Education	10.67

TABLE -3.9
ACCORDING TO LEVELS OF QUALIFICATIONS OF WOMEN

Level	*Per cent*
Doctorate degree holder	1.24
Post graduate	15.76
Graduate	57.38
Diploma holders in technical & professional field	14.03
Others like ITI certificate holders.	11.59

TABLE - 3.10
ENGINEERING & TECHNOLOGY

Qualification	Salary Slab	Male Pub.	Male Pvt.	Female Pub.	Female Pvt.
Ph.D	500-1000	19	3	6	0
	1000-1500	116	12	20	0
	1500-2000	455	102	7	0
	2000-3000	1049	159	4	1
	3000 & above	132	166	1	0
	Combined	2011	523	39	3
P.G. Degree	500-1000	331	114	18	6
	1000-1500	2404	621	43	12
	1500-2000	3410	849	56	4
	2000-3000	3348	1121	18	3
	3000 & above	507	1013	2	2
	Combined	11283	4471	168	44
P.G. Diploma	500-1000	483	162	61	19
	1000-1500	658	277	22	4
	1500-2000	681	202	18	2
	2000-3000	754	253	1	1
	3000 & above	219	259	1	11
	Combined	3190	1376	124	64
Graduate	500-1000	11152	2756	255	108
	1000-1500	26614	5616	302	80
	1500-2000	21209	4709	140	55
	2000-3000	15218	5472	67	26
	3000 & above	2121	3878	14	14
	Combined	87696	27769	905	396
Undergraduate	500-1000	49911	8127	1172	327
	1000-1500	34753	6658	320	55
	1500-2000	10487	3121	60	26
	2000-3000	2773	2276	5	16
	3000 & above	452	967	11	5
	Combined	123141	29090	1994	907
Combined	500-1000	61987	11184	1514	461
	1000-1500	64621	13202	707	151
	1500-2000	36266	8987	281	87
	2000-3000	23149	9284	95	47
	3000 & above	3434	6286	29	32
	Combined	227566	63298	3233	1415

TABLE - 3.11
GENDERWISE EMPLOYMENT SCENARIO IN SCIENTIFIC ESTABLISHMENTS

			Male		*Female*	
Field	*Qualification*	*Salary Slab*	*Pub.*	*Pvt.*	*Pub.*	*Pvt.*
Veterinary Science	P.G. Degree	500-1000	181	12	16	1
		1000-1500	539	24	11	0
		1500-2000	420	16	6	1
		2000-3000	121	15	0	0
		3000 & above	3	9	0	0
		Combined	1457	100	33	2
	Graduate	500-1000	1795	48	35	0
		1000-1500	3846	200	30	1
		1500-2000	1161	61	6	0
		2000-3000	138	80	0	0
		3000 & above	28	45	0	0
		Combined	8440	546	81	3
	Combined	500-1000	2328	81	51	1
		1000-1500	4650	236	42	1
		1500-2000	1944	83	13	1
		2000-3000	392	104	1	0
		3000 & above	28	60	0	0
		Combined	11343	728	125	5
Science	Ph.D	500-1000	276	100	93	30
		1000-1500	1695	433	373	104
		1500-2000	2867	668	306	42
		2000-3000	2338	266	126	21
		3000 & above	203	174	1	7
		Combined	8501	1987	1035	294
	P.G. Degree	500-1000	16205	3969	2906	1324
		1000-1500	13605	5280	1854	1291
		1500-2000	9057	3935	780	544
		2000-3000	4424	1077	172	36
		3000 & above	598	517	53	7
		Combined	54265	19587	7579	4681
	Graduate	500-1000	65694	15923	10826	2090
		1000-1500	28417	7692	2513	464
		1500-2000	12671	3993	552	157
		2000-3000	6656	3015	267	61
		3000 & above	1239	1447	37	40
		Combined	147573	48193	18889	6212

(Contd.)

Field	Qualification	Salary Slab	Male Pub.	Male Pvt.	Female Pub.	Female Pvt.
	Combined	500-1000	82636	20097	13914	3496
		1000-1500	44092	13510	4777	1874
		1500-2000	24854	8642	1645	747
		2000-3000	13617	4385	568	126
		3000 & above	2060	2161	91	54
	Combined	Combined	211923	70165	27673	11316
Agricultural Science	Ph.D.	500-1000	38	2	0	0
		1000-1500	317	20	8	0
		1500-2000	751	28	10	0
		2000-3000	653	32	3	0
		3000 & above	37	21	0	0
		Combined	1966	145	27	0
	P.G. Degree	500-1000	1973	152	22	6
		1000-1500	3034	181	36	0
		1500-2000	2229	140	20	0
		2000-3000	873	58	1	6
		3000 & above	57	24	0	1
		Combined	9731	786	92	24
	Graduate	500-1000	8686	1118	111	9
		1000-1500	8346	611	65	1
		1500-2000	2820	275	32	0
		2000-3000	729	152	2	0
		3000 & above	80	66	0	5
		Combined	26344	3384	253	18
	Combined	500-1000	11293	1318	137	15
		1000-1500	11871	826	111	1
		1500-2000	5884	451	62	1
		2000-3000	2290	249	6	6
		3000 & above	175	117	0	6
		Combined	39464	579	43	

It appears that women were reluctant to take up the work like construction, industrial production, marketing, etc., as their percentage in these activities was found less than two, whereas the percentage of men was high as 176.

22 per cent women and 18% men were in administrative jobs.

21 per cent women and 15% men were in consultation.

For S&T Personnel

Women are not included to join the manufacturing industries. Only 4 per cent of them compared to 20 per cent of men were employed in such organizations.

The preference of women in terms of organizations for employment has been teaching institutions, medical & finance and insurance organizations. In teaching institutions, women were 45.8 per cent whereas percentage of men were 18.8 per cent.

In medical institutions and hospitals, women were 22.1 per cent compared to 10.6 per cent of men.

The female percentage among scientific and technical (S&T) personnel was found to be 14.78 per cent.

About two-thirds of S&T personnel were engaged in some sort of jobs and one-tenth of them were women. 17.36 per cent of male and 43.19 per cent of females were engaged in teaching. In R & D activities, male and female percentage was 11.33 and 5.46 respectively.

A survey of employed females shows that as a group, women hold very different attitude and expectations towards work. Women who shared certain personal traits and who were in the same occupation tended to be quite similar in their attitudes towards work, working women in blue-collar jobs were much more likely than those in other occupations show need for higher income. Women in service jobs were second highest in preference for higher income. Female clerical staff were more inclined to get promotion, and those in technical jobs prefer meaningful work. These results could be analysed on the basis of Maslow's need hierarchy theory and they are most useful in developing enlightened personnel policies and motivation strategies in organizations.

Women at Work: Myths versus Reality

Discrimination against females in employment and promotion is often subtle since so many of our attitudes and stereotypes about women have been conditioned in our personality since childhood. Discrimination in this context refers to non-job related limitations. It is often seen that there is rejection of women's applications for non-job related reasons, and often recruited women are for certain position at lower salaries, representing some form of discrimination. Some of the myths about working women and their corresponding realities need clarification.

A myth is that a woman's place is in her home and she devotes her time there but the reality is that home making is no longer a full time job for most women because of smaller family norms, nuclear families, changing attitudes and entry of technology to kitchens. Today more than half of all women between 18 and 64 years of age are in labour force making substantial contribution to nations economy. In reality they are making significant contribution.

Another myth is that women fall ill more often than male workers. So it adds cost to the company. But a recent study shows that there is little difference in absenteeism rate due to illness or injury between male and female workers.

Myth is that women don't work as long or as regularly as their male counterparts and their training is costly and largely wasted. It is true that a number of women leave work after marriage and children but a majority return when their children are in school. Even with a break in employment the average woman worker has a work life expectancy of 25 years, as compared with 43 years for the average male worker. This reality is embedded into social reality and women cannot be discounted for this.

The deep-rooted belief is that women should stick to 'women's job' and should not try to step up or compete with men's jobs. This sounds absolutely baseless because job requirement with extremely rare exception are related to sex. Tradition and stereotypes rather than job content has led to labelling of certain jobs for women and others for men.

Another myth is the belief that women don't want responsibility on the job, they want promotion. The truth is that very few women have been given jobs of responsibility but when given opportunities, women like men, do cope with job responsibilities in addition to personal or family responsibility.

It is also a common myth that men don't like to work under women supervisors. The reality is that most men who complain about women supervisors have perhaps never worked under a woman. In a recent study about men who had worked under women managers report that their evaluation of women in management has been favourable.

Only certain occupations are appropriate for women. However cultures vary in what they consider as appropriate work for women.

Job segregation is so extensive in most part of the globe. 50 per cent of women are often employed in women type jobs.

Looking at Indian Scenario

Main conclusions from 1981 census of technical personnel working women and their job:

1. The female percentage among scientific and technical (S&T) personnel was found to be 14.78 per cent.
2. About two-thirds of S&T personnel were engaged in some sort of jobs and one-tenth of them were women.
3. 17.36 percentage of male and 43.19 percentage of female were engaged in teaching.
4. In Research and Development activities, male-female percentage was 11.33 and 5.46 respectively.
5. It appears that women were reluctant to take up work in construction, industrial production, marketing, etc., as their percentage indicates whereas percentage of men was 17.
6. 22 per cent women and 18 per cent men were in administrative jobs.
7. 21 per cent women and 15 per cent men were in consultation.
8. Women are not inclined to join the manufacturing industries. Only 4 per cent of them, compared to 20 per cent of mén, were employed in such organization.
9. The preference of women in terms of organizations for employment has been teaching institutions, mechanical, finance and insurance organizations.
10. In teaching institutions, women were 45.8 per cent, whereas percentage of men was 18.8 per cent.
11. In mechanical institutions and hospitals women were 22.1 per cent compared to 10.6 per cent men.
12. The growth rate of scientific and technical personnel has been 3.6 times from 1961 to 1971 and 1.9 times from 1971 to 1981.
13. Employment had increased by 2.8 times from 1961 to 1971 and 1-7 times from 1971 to 1981.

14. Employment in government section increased by 2-8 times from 1961 to 1971 and 1-8 times from 1971 to 1981.
15. Ratio of employment in government sector was 58.12 per cent in 1961; 45.79 per cent in 1971 and 44.57 per cent in 1981.
16. 8.6 per cent were self-employed in 1961, 7.27 per cent in 1971 and 8.56 per cent in 1981. In terms of actual strength the number of self-employed increased by 2.8 times from 1961 to 1971 and 2.3 times from 1971 to 1981.
17. Unemployment increased by 5.8 times from 1961 to 1971 and 2-3 times from 1971 to 1981. In terms of percentage, unemployment was 10.12 per cent in 1961, 16.9 per cent in 1971 and in 1981 survey the unemployment among S&T personnel was 21.31per cent.

Source: 1981 Census of Technical Personnel.

Work Involvement, Competitiveness Relationships

Women were found to be professionally assertive, but less competitive. This, however, does not affect their productivity. In a study of equally productive men and women, the causes of motivation were entirely different as discussed earlier in this chapter.

There are attitudes that work as dominant factors affecting work life it is believed that it is disgraceful for a man to be a woman's subordinate. There is nothing technical or professional in this attitude, but organizational productivity might suffer. Work groups should be composed of either sex but never of both sexes is another belief. This is again untrue. The matter is further complicated by the fact that neither of these attitudes and prejudices are isolated. This creates a complex set of reactions at the place of work. The psychologists and more recently sociologists Mead have brought out implications of female control to which every male is subjected to from birth to adolescence. The refusal to be subordinate to women thus might appear as a compensation for degree of subordination during the early years of life.

It is observed that men accept women as superior with great reluctance and the channels of vertical mobility are not open to women. The reasons for man's discomfort with women at work may also be due to the fact that men have an unconscious fear of being overshadowed by a woman. Seniority rules also have implications. Since they are normally made in such a way so as to give weight to continuity of employment which places women at a disadvantage. The career cycle, in spite of allowances for maternity, does not allow woman to compete with men in terms of occupational continuity because a working woman is also invariably incharge of the household activities and child care which is equally taxing as the work outside. Women have to work under these two pressures. The working capacity of a woman thus appears to be greater than that of men. Thus there is an urgent need to change the human resource policies.

Women owned businesses form only a small fraction of the total businesses in India. Out of women's businesses, about 90% of them are service related and only 7% are in manufacturing and finance in high technology areas like computer software.

A female entrepreneur is usually over thirty-five years of age, married and well settled. For the women who fit into the above profile, being married and having a family provides emotional and financial support to launch an endeavour. Balancing the dual roles the family and business can create stressful situations, which requires superior organization skills. It may be interesting to note that politics as a career naturally comes to men with early associations whereas women generally join politics after the age of forty. As a result, work and family are often into available fragments of time, during which the women's mind is totally free from either of them.

This section has attempted to present an Indian scenario of 'women and work'. The next chapter presents a research study of women doctors, engineers and architects of Delhi.

FOUR

Occupational Choices and Life of Professional Women

Family support, education, family background, practical aspects, social norms and attitudes, role models, parental attitudes and perception of working women are some of the correlates of career choices and career development of women. In this section these issues are presented through a survey of women doctors, engineers and architects of Delhi. The study is a part of work sponsored by the Department of Science and Technology, Government of India and has been completed in 1997.

It may be interesting to note here that there are a number of theories of occupational choices in the literature of organizational psychology and human resource management, which suggest that these choices reflect basic personal orientations, derived from child rearing practices. Bailyn and Scheing found a pattern of occupational type which reflected both background factors and current values. Career theory attempts to relate personal orientations more directly to occupational environment in terms of six basic dimensions. These are realistic, intellectual, social, conventional, enterprising and artistic. Super and Bohn postulated that career development is essentially a process of synthesis of the person's self-concept with the realities of the external environment. Studies also show that women's perception of work and satisfaction are different than that of men.

The issue of occupational choice is important from Human Resources Management and Development perspectives too. Encyclopaedia of women's studies highlights further aspects of the issues. Development of database on women with science and technology education will unfold many aspects of the issues of development, work designs and women's studies, with reference to science and technology education.

Career Choice and Development

In the forties and fifties, 50% of the girls entered medicine with service motive, about 41% for economic independence and about 7% for prestige reasons. During the sixties and seventies, prestige and family traditions are quoted as reasons influencing girls for choosing medical career and hardly 5-10% give service as a motive. The recent trend seems to be that the appeal of the profession and employment opportunities available influence the career choice. The career choice is mostly self-choice and much influenced by the parents. There are innumerable barriers in the career development of women. These are largely attitude related social, psychological and organizational factors.

The traditional Indian values expect women to be subordinate, altruistic and self-sacrificing. But the qualities, needed in work life are competition, confidence and assurance. In Indian families, boys are encouraged and reinforced to develop masculine characteristics—aggression, dominance, independence, sense of adventure and achievement oriented; whereas girls are encouraged to acquire feminine characteristics such as being submissive, nurturing, dependant and less achievement oriented. It is also true that girls are brought up with marriage as the goal of life and not career. The studies also report that women physicians did not have a straight career path as men physicians had and they could not sustain their early accomplishments. By mid career, they are generally lazy behind men with similar initial performance. The reasons are found to be that the priority given to family demands were barriers to career development Kalarani (1976), Lebra (1984), and Sinha (1989). Women had to accommodate to husband's career's and had to opt for positions compatible with their family roles. Kapur (1984) and Sinha (1987). Many Indian women refused transfers, promotion, etc., as they did not want to move out and get separated from their families Ramu (1977). As the families do not permit women to live alone, spatial mobility gets reduced Bluemberg and Dwarki, (1982). Her personal safety and security is in danger Lebra (1984) and her chastity is questioned (Chaturvedi 1985; Srivastava) 1986).

Due to women's preoccupation with marriage, family and child care responsibilities, career development is affected and this results in role strain and role conflict and sometimes they sacrifice career for family.

In spite of all these barriers, the research also reports that married women doctors did better than unmarried ones especially in establishing dispensaries, hospitals and private practice due to their choice of specialization which was either in terms of women and childrens' diseases such as gynaecology, obstetrics, paediatrics or non-clinical specialities such as physiology, anatomy or pathology so that there would be fixed hours of duty, less tension and more compatibility to adjust to the family roles. Those women physicians who married physicians expressed husband's positive attitude and support in having joint practice. American studies also confirm most of the findings of the Indian studies regarding career development. It is also found that there is more rigid gender typing of specialities in the USA, the typical women's speciality being paediatrics and typical men's speciality being surgery (Elston, 1980; Rosenthal, 1979). In the US, among practising women physicians, in 1985, 68% worked in primary care fields; internal medicine family and general practice, obstetrics and gynaecology, paediatrics or psychiatry. In contrast, only 44% of male physicians practised in these specialities (Martin, Parker and Arnold, 1987). As domestic help is very expensive, American women have more career interruptions; despite good performance and high grades in medical schools and internships at prestigious teaching hospitals, women physicians did not sustain their early accomplishments. By mid-career, their professional attainment lagged behind men with similar initial performance. Heins (1976) reports that women physicians suffered from role overload, role conflict and felt that they had too many demands on their time and energy and hence very little time for themselves. Data from 1986 shows that only 52% of the women physicians were self-employed in contrast to 77% men physicians. Women physicians averaged 73000 dollars annual net income compared to 1,18,000 dollars by men.

Career Performance

Most of the studies from the countries on women professionals, in general, report that the aspiration level of women is not very high and that is the reason why most women end up at middle level leadership and hardly 1% rise from that up. Women are quite satisfied with their achievements even if they do not rise to the top. They are not too much concerned about salary or promotion and are more interested with the atmosphere of the workplace, and personal relationships. If self-employed, women work less number of hours than men.

The medical work ratio of, full time equated months in medical work since medical school graduation is calculated as 0.993 for men and for women it is 0.880 women work less number of hours, about 70% of men's time and the median personal income is in the proportion of 40 : 60. Women physicians with children do show fewer hours worked and more career interruptions than male physicians but the overall or after time productivity is not that much lower. But professional productivity is not always the most significant factor influencing professional status.

Sinha, Kapur and Horner attribute women physician's lack of representation at the top levels of medical institutions to their modest ambition.

Studies which tested for success avoidance in women found many situations in which women were ambitious, especially in advancement in their own fields. Research on women in male dominated fields found that women could be equally competitive with men, given the right work environment (Kanter, Epestein, Mathuchidambaram, Oomen Dubey).

In India, women physicians who enter service either with Government institutions work full time and as there is a salary scale, earn the same as men. But in private practice, they earn less due to their speciality, hours worked and the number of patients seen. In specialities like general surgery, cardiology, neuro surgery, etc., which are male dominated, men earn much more. 85% of the Indian women, prefer to consult women physicians unless there is an emergency.

In the USA, it is found that 58% men and 49% women prefer to consult male physicians and 40% have no preference for men or women physicians. One of the studies on preference reported that the respondents felt that women were more sensitive, more caring, more sympathetic, better in communicating, they had better rapport and they were respectful of patients' concerns whereas men were more assertive and cut and ignored patients' questions.

Career development of male physicians follows a progressive direct line with many factors contributing to professional attainment. The factors identified are achievement motivation, medical school performance, faculty and peer recognition in medical school, internship location and family responsibilities. For women physicians, in spite of all academic parameters such as academic performance, award of honours and prestigious residences, being equal, because of family responsibilities, their scholarly productivity is less than men. Women physicians publish fewer papers than men; they are less mobile which is necessary for succeeding in academics. Women belong to professional organizations and they are more active in attending meetings.

Though there have been increases in the number of women employed full time in medical school faculties, in promotion to assistant professors and substantial increases of women in academic administration, still, not many women head medical colleges world wide, including Russia where 75% of the physicians are women.

Professional Role Performance

Stereotypical physicians are supposed to have characteristics such as rationality, objectivity, technical authoritativeness and aggressiveness in face of emergencies. Women physicians are supposed to embody characteristics such as compassion, personal involvement, patience and maternal authoritativeness. Whether women are a small or large percentage of physicians, the gender concentration in the different specialities is remarkably consistent from country to country with paediatrics, the typical women's speciality and surgery the typical men's. In Asia, Latin America and the Middle East, more women specialize in gynaecology because of the modesty of female patients in these countries.

Due to sex typing the sex role expectation of the society on one hand and rights and duties expected from the professionals occupying a certain place in the hierarchy of the organization there is conflict between the occupational role expectation and feminine role expectation.

As women's role is associated with home making, bearing

and rearing of children and hence with attributes such as warmth, patience, empathy, grace, endurance, etc., they are tracked into lower prestige work and not considered leadership material (Lober, Osaka, Venkatarathnam, Martin and Osmond, etc.).

If a woman is successful in her occupation she is less successful as a woman (Muthuchidambaram, 1990, Brown and Kliein, 1982) as there is incongruence between occupational role expectations and feminine role expectations. Sex role, sex role expectations and sex segregation do effect the professional performance of women physicians.

The Global Scenario

Comparing figures with those of other countries, we find in technically advanced United States of America working women comprised fewer than 1% in 1960 (Robin, 1960).

In the mid seventies women entered engineering in significant numbers and by 1979, 9 per cent of the Bachelor's degree recipients were women (Sheridan, 1980) and by 1985, the number of women has increased to 14%. There were more women in medicine and law than in engineering.

Women in England held high positions in science and technology even in 1964 and they had received recognition for their scientific achievements. The number of women in engineering and technology in the USSR was about 30% of the total number of engineers; in Norway it was 9.8%, in Sweden 9.4%, in Federal Republic of Germany 4% and in the Middle East 9.5%.

A review of the studies done on women professionals in general and women engineers in particular by scholars in India and abroad and a synthesis of the findings give us the picture described in the following pages.

There is only a small number of women in the profession of engineering due to three reasons, says Ressie Barnard.

1. The attitude that engineering is an all male profession and therefore girls are counselled away from it.
2. Unwillingness of employers to hire women, as they fear that they would lose them after they marry.
3. Several obstacles arising from sex difference in engineering work.

Studies done in India state that engineering education is generally a long and expensive course. Parents in India naturally prefer to spend their scarce resources to support their sons in engineering college. Many parents think that money spent on engineering education of the daughter brings no return to the family as she has to be married off. As a result, women students form a tiny percentage of the total strength in engineering colleges.

Other prejudices are that women do not have the stamina to pursue engineering studies and that they do not have the adequate talent for mathematics which is the basis for engineering studies.

Studies also reveal that in the early stages women from upper middle-class families, with consistent high academic record, joined engineering colleges in India. They belonged to high income groups and had educated parents. Usually the father was the role model. During the fifties and sixties, mostly Christian and Hindu girls from the forward caste took advantage of engineering studies. During the seventies and eighties, Hindu girls from backward communities as well as Muslim girls started entering engineering institutions. But even in the eighties, 83% of the girls entering engineering college were from urban areas and only 17% came from rural areas (Muthuchidambaram, 1990). Majority of the fathers were graduates and postgraduates and 3% of them were engineers themselves. During the eighties about 28% of the mothers of the engineering college girl students were working women, 23% of the mothers were graduates, 75% were matriculates and hardly 3% were uneducated. This confirms the findings of the earlier studies on women professionals by Blumberg and Dwaraka Prasad, Krishnamurari, Chaturvedi, Pandey, Gore, etc. That there was high correlation between education of parents and the level of educational attainment of their daughters. Parents played a dominant role in setting the educational goals for their children. The girls, when they finished school, were hardly 15-16 years of age and quite immature. They did not have adequate career information or vocational guidance, had limited exposure, had no role models and held the value of obeying the parents and let them choose their careers themselves.

Career Choice

Parental encouragement and marks obtained in the qualifying examination decided their entry into engineering courses.

Career choices and career decisions are influenced by the decisions about marriage, parenthood, female-male responsibilities in home making, social norms and expected sex roles, women are not free to explore their interest and make choice conscious perspective. In most of the Indian families, even today, girls are not taken seriously when it is a matter of career and it is considered to be of secondary importance. Marriage is still, the principal determinant of women's social position. Sex role stereotyping influences women's lives from birth and it is a powerful influence in schools. This results in restrictions upon the freedom of occupational choice and career development of girls.

Currently the factors due to which girls take to engineering and technology are the social status and prestige, which goes with the profession and economic independence it would bring to them. This finding of Muthuchidambaram (1990) is supported by the findings of Horst (1981) who listed the factors of career choice in order of importance. The chance to earn good money, attaining social status and prestige, to look forward to a stable secure future and to use one's special abilities were cited as important reasons for choosing engineering studies.

Another common finding is that the role model of women who choose engineering was mostly the father and in the USA most of the women engineers during the seventies had fathers who were engineers themselves, according to Horst (1981).

In India as well as USA and UK, the government are following an aggressive policy to attract more women into non-traditional jobs in engineering sciences. This is also one of the main reasons which encourage women to choose engineering.

Career Development

Women's career development depends on a number of factors. Due to women's preoccupation with marriage, family and child care responsibilities, there is role strain which leads to role conflict thus effecting the career. Usually career development is assessed in terms of promotion of higher cadres, improvement in knowledge and specialization in the profession.

In the case of women engineers it is found that career options are restricted by the employment agency itself. There is reluctance on the part of private industries to employ women in their undertakings. Hence most of the women engineering graduates choose to join the government or quasi-government organizations or trust organizations. Women prefer government organizations as there is security of regulations; the only snag is that it is a transferable service. Many Indian women engineers, after marriage used to drop out of service in the seventies, some studies have also reported that they refuse promotions if they are transferred as they do not like to relocate. Unmarried women have more geographical, mobility to avail better opportunities but they do not like to be alone on their own, as their personal safety and security is in danger (Blumberg and Dwaraka (1980), Bebra (1980)).

Due to sex typing of the profession, 58% of the women used to choose Civil Engineering and they preferred desk work such as designing and drafting as it was considered that women were not tough enough to manage men workers in construction work. Less than 5% of the women engineers are found.

Attitudes of Women Physicians

American studies found that women physicians were generally more liberal and egalitarian than men physicians. Older women were more liberal than older men and younger men were closer in attitudes to young women. Egalitarian included attitudes about equality in occupations, domestic responsibilities, domestic decision making and appropriate gender role behaviour. Liberalism included attitudes towards reducing costs for patients, positive attitudes towards welfare policies such as maternity leave, part time internship, etc., racial tolerance, liberal sex role orientation, efforts to overcome race and sex discrimination, banning of nuclear weapons, aborting laws, pre-marital sex, etc.

Regarding the attitudes of Indian women physicians towards social issues, Indian studies report that women physicians are found to be positive in their attitude towards women's movement, concept of equality of both sexes, prohibition of dowry, property rights for women, intercaste marriage, widow remarriage, legalization of abortion and liberal sex role orientation thus confirming that they are rational in their thinking.

Conclusion

There has been a striking demographic shift in the profession of medicine. 35% of all physicians in India are women. Women now practice in virtually every medical speciality though the traditional difference in the choice of speciality still continues. The number of women entering medical profession is increasing but their accession to senior faculty positions has not kept pace. They lack role models and mentors. Women physicians are struggling to combine a medical career with raising a family. Subtle forms of sex discrimination still remains active. Research on women in male dominated fields found that women could be equally competitive with men, given the right environment. Persistent and pervasive gender discrimination rooted in the status of women in male dominated society still keeps women in the lower or middle level careers in spite of their competence and capability.

Better networking, patronage and sponsorship and higher visibility are needed for women to be successful in their career. Whatever the obstacles, women are found to perform as well as men; the percentage of women entering surgery and surgical specialities has increased; the number of women in medical school faculties has increased. There has been substantial increase in the number of women in academic administration. Recent pressures against sex discrimination has brought about positive changes. Support structures such as reliable child care services, hostels for working women, subsidized health care, creches, day-care centres, senior citizens hostels, social security measures, etc., are recommended to help the women physicians in executing their occupation roles better.

Women Engineers and Architects

History and Related Studies

Engineering education in India was started in late the eighteenth century. An engineering school was started in Madras in 1774 and it was upgraded into a college in 1847. College was started in 1847 at Roorkee, Calcutta Engineering College in 1856 and Indian Institute at Bangalore in 1911. At the time of our independence, there were 38 Engineering Colleges with 2940 students and by 1957, the number of responsibility and they try to manage their aims with the help of hired servant or family members. They do feel guilty of neglecting their homes and children. The family career conflicts among all working women is a worldwide phenomenon. Women engineers, because of these dual career problems, choose jobs which are not too demanding, with regular working hours, less travelling, etc., and consequently end up in lower prestige work, earning less salary.

Attitudes of Women Engineers

The adjectives for women engineers which got the highest ranks are reliable, independent, adaptable and aggressive in a study by Horst (1982). The trend seems to be that women engineers in USA, with their high intellectual ability, energy, motivation and extreme independence are competing successfully with their male counterparts. Among all professionals, women engineers give more support for 'feminism'. They are more optimistic in their belief to equal pay or equal work. They have more egalitarian relationship with men, more liberal in their perception of sex role orientation. There is an increasing level of confidence among women engineers and the growing emphasis seems to be on career rather than family.

Indian women engineers have been found to be positive in their attitude towards equality of sexes, prohibition of dowry, effective enforcement of the laws, concerning prevention of violence against women such as rape, cruelty to widows, child abuse, prostitution, etc.

Conclusion

In the course of the last 40 years, there has been a dramatic change in the attitude of the people in allowing girls to take up professions like Engineering. In India, in 1951 there were hardly 19 girl students in the Engineering faculty and today there are more than 12000 women enrolled in the engineering institutions. It is the same in other countries as well. More and more middle income families are taking advantage of professional education and this is a means of upward social mobility. More women are interested in combining employment with marital and family commitments as women are entering the so called non-traditional careers and engineering seems as a prototype for all traditionally male professions. Many situational barriers and interpersonal barriers have been identified and all studies document the pervasive nature of discrimination against women in several settings. But studies have also noted the increasing level of confidence among the women engineers and most of the women are there because of the satisfaction they derive and the sense of achievement they get out of the work. There is considerable room for professional opportunities and growth if one has the ability. One of the engineering managers made a remark that is a fitting conclusion. He says "I hire brains not gender". According to Erick Erickson, women have to learn "how to be women and workers, wives and colleagues, mothers and creative beings and have a sense of continuity". Engineering and science are well apart from workers sex differences.

Rajeswari and Samadhanam's data book gives details on science and technology manpower of India, quality of work life and work psychology, etc. The questions were both objective and subjective. Few questions were also framed, keeping in mind diversity of scope in their respective fields and responses.

The variables of the study are:

1. Background variables (family description, etc.)
2. Personal variables (salary, education, etc.)
3. Academic variables (schooling and technical education)
4. Socio-cultural variables (attitudes, values).
5. Self-concept (perception of self)
6. Quality of work life perception (attitude of management, etc).
7. Work psychology variable (motivation, expectation, satisfaction, evaluation, etc.)
8. General aspects (reasons for low representation of women, etc.)
9. Occupational choices and occupational patterns.

Data Collection

The questionnaires were mailed to 512 respondents in Delhi, along with self-addressed envelops. The response was not very encouraging. As in the first 15 days there were hardly two or three replies and by the end of the first month the response picked up. By the middle of second month it almost stopped. Only 45% of the questionnaires were returned by the respondents. Then an effort was made to contact professionals individually. The response was encouraging and we were able to collect the required data for the project work, though it had taken little more time than expected.

TABLE - 4.1
BREAK UP OF THE RESPONDENTS

(Total Sample N = 300)

Category	*No. of response*
P.G. Students	70
Practising Professionals	180
Others	50
	300

However the respondents differed in different groups.

This section presents the data analysis of personal background, sociological, psychological, occupational and work design factors of women with technology education. In this study, women engineers, architects and doctors of Delhi have been included. Part A presents the data analysis for engineers. Part B is about architects and Part C about doctors. The subsections for each group are presented under background variables, academic life, perception of self, occupational pattern, quality of work life, socio-cultural attitudes and general opinion. Analysis is presented in terms of percentages.

Women Engineers of Delhi

Background Variables

The age distribution, birth order and family details of the respondents are presented in tables 4.2 to 4.14. It is seen that the percentage of women above age of 30 is 52 per cent as compared to 48 per cent in age group below 30. Most of them belong to small families having not more than one brother (31%) or sister (28%). Most of them belong to highly qualified families in which either parents are graduates. Further, 67 per cent of the father's are post-graduates. It is evident from the data that the respondents who are married have their spouses from equally qualified backgrounds. The data given below present the educational level of father, mother, sister, brother, husband, mother in-law, father in-law.

Table 4.2 represents the age of the respondents. 12 per cent of the respondents are below 25 years, 36 per cent are in the age group of 25-30 years and rest 52 per cent are in category of 31 years and above.

TABLE - 4.2
AGE OF THE RESPONDENTS

Age Group	*Per cent*
Below 25 years	12.0
25-30 years	36.0
31 and above	52.0
	100.0

Table 4.3 represents the birth order of the respondents. 37 per cent of the respondents belong to 'only child' family background.

TABLE - 4.3
BIRTH ORDER OF THE RESPONDENTS

Birth Order	*Per cent*
Only child	37.0
Eldest child	27.0
Middle child	27.0
Last child	7.0
Any other	2.0
	100.0

Table 4.4 gives the number of brothers of the respondents. 41 per cent of the respondents don't have any brother, whereas 59 per cent have one or more brothers.

TABLE - 4.4
NUMBER OF BROTHERS OF THE RESPONDENTS

Brother	*Per cent*
0	41.0
1	31.0
2	14.0
3	8.0
4	6.0
	100.0

Table 4.5 shows that 37% of the respondents do not have any sister, 28% of them have one sister, 22% have two sisters.

TABLE - 4.5
NUMBER OF SISTERS OF THE RESPONDENTS

Sister	*Per cent*
0	37.0
1	28.0
2	22.0
3	9.0
4	4.0
	100.0

Table 4.6 gives mother's education of the respondents. The data clearly shows that 49% of the mothers have graduate degree and 30% of them are postgraduates.

TABLE - 4.6
MOTHER'S EDUCATION

Education	*Per cent*
Lower	6.0
High School	15.0
Graduate	49.0
Postgraduate	30.0
	100.0

Table 4.7 shows that 67% of the respondent fathers are postgraduates and 26% are graduates and only 3% are high school pass outs.

TABLE - 4.7
FATHER'S EDUCATION

Education	*Per cent*
No Reply	4.0
High School	3.0
Graduate	26.0
Postgraduate	67.0
	100.0

Table 4.8 gives the educational level of sister. The data shows that only 24% of the respondents have postgraduate sisters.

TABLE. - 4.8
EDUCATIONAL LEVEL OF SISTER (ONE)

Education	*Per cent*
No Reply	53.0
High School	6.0
Graduate	17.0
Postgraduate	24.0
	100.0

Table 4.9 gives the educational level of sister. 72% of the respondents don't have more than one sibling. Out of 28% of the respondents who have more than one sibling 21% are postgraduates and 6% of them are graduates.

TABLE - 4.9
EDUCATIONAL LEVEL OF SISTER (TWO)

Education	*Per cent*
No Reply	72.0
High School	1.0
Graduate	6.0
Postgraduate	21.0
	100.0

Table 4.10 gives the educational level of brothers. 50% of them don't have any brother, 28% of the brothers are postgraduates and 20% of them are graduates.

TABLE - 4.10
EDUCATIONAL LEVEL OF BROTHER (ONE)

Education	*Per cent*
No Reply	50.0
High School	2.0
Graduate	20.0
Postgraduate	28.0
	100.0

Table 4.11 gives the educational level of second brother. Again 62% of them don't have any brother, 21% of the brothers are graduates and 15% of them are postgraduates.

TABLE - 4.11
EDUCATIONAL LEVEL OF BROTHER (TWO)

Education	*Per cent*
No Reply	62.0
High School	2.0
Graduate	21.0
Postgraduate	15.0
	100.0

The educational level of respondents husband is given in Table 4.12. 30% of the respondents didn't reply. The data reveals that 50% of the husbands are postgraduates and 20% are graduates.

TABLE - 4.12
EDUCATIONAL LEVEL OF HUSBAND

Education	*Per cent*
No Reply	30.0
High School	0.0
Graduate	20.0
Postgraduate	50.0
	100.0

Table 4.13 presents the educational level of mother-in-law. Only 5% have done postgraduation and 21% are graduates and 27% have studied till high school level.

TABLE - 4.13
EDUCATIONAL LEVEL OF MOTHER IN-LAW

Education	*Per cent*
No Reply	37.0
Lower School	10.0
High School	27.0
Graduate	21.0
Postgraduate	5.0
	100.0

Table 4.14 represents educational level of father-in-law of the respondents. 45% of them are graduates and 16% of them are post-graduates. Only 12% have studied till high school level.

TABLE - 4.14
EDUCATIONAL LEVEL OF FATHER IN-LAW

Education	*Per cent*
No Reply	27.0
High School	12.0
Graduate	45.0
Postgraduate	16.0
	100.0

Table 4.15 gives data regarding respondents husband's profession. 42% of them are from engineering background, 10% are from medical and rest from other fields. Tables 4.15 to 4.28 present the data on the professional background and occupation of the respondents and their families. 37% of the respondents' fathers are with engineering background and respondents who are married have husbands (42%) from the same profession. Brothers and sisters are also with the professional background. 72% of the respondents' fathers and 47% of the respondents' husbands are working either with private organizations or government organizations. Very few are doing their own business. 6% in the case of spouses and 4% in the case of fathers, 51% of the mothers of the respondents are housewives. 46% of the mothers of the respondents had social science background.

TABLE - 4.15
HUSBAND'S PROFESSION

Profession	*Per cent*
No Reply	28.0
Medical	10.0
Engineering	42.0
Teaching	2.0
Social Sciences	9.0
Science	7.0
Others	2.0
	100.0

Table 4.16 gives father's profession. Again it is evident that engineering remains the main profession in their choice of career. 37% are engineers, 26% are doctors, 15% have social science background and 11% are from sciences.

TABLE - 4.16
FATHER'S PROFESSION

Profession	*Per cent*
No Reply	7.0
Medical	26.0
Engineering	37.0
Social Sciences	15.0
Science	11.0
Others	4.0
	100.0

Table 4.17 gives mother's profession of the respondents. As contrast to their husbands background, the majority of the mothers are from social sciences background, i.e., 46% of the mothers, 20% are with science background and 7% and 2% with engineering or medical respectively.

TABLE - 4.17
MOTHER'S PROFESSION

Profession	*Per cent*
No Reply	22.0
Medical	2.0
Engineering	7.0
Social Sciences	46.0
Science	20.0
Others	3.0
	100.0

As regarding the profession of the sisters the Tables 4.18 and 4.19 show that there is no clear preference as far as their professions are concerned, only 9% and 3% are with medical background, 6% and 5% are engineers, 29% and 4% are with social science background.

TABLE - 4.18
PROFESSION OF THE SISTER (ONE)

Profession	*Per cent*
No Reply	47.0
Medical	9.0
Engineering	6.0
Social Sciences	2.0
Science	29.0
Others	7.0
	100.0

TABLE - 4.19
PROFESSION OF THE SISTER (TWO)

Profession	*Per cent*
No Reply	81.0
Medical	3.0
Engineering	5.0
Social Sciences	1.0
Science	4.0
Others	6.0
	100.0

Tables 4.20 and 4.21 give a detailed picture of brothers profession. Like sisters, the percentage of brothers choices are divided into different fields. Major choice remains engineering and science.

TABLE - 4.20
PROFESSION OF THE BROTHER (ONE)

Profession	*Per cent*
No Reply	51.0
Medical	12.0
Engineering	16.0
Social Sciences	3.0
Science	13.0
Others	5.0
	100.0

TABLE - 4.21
PROFESSION OF THE BROTHER (TWO)

Profession	*Per cent*
No Reply	81.0
Agriculture	2.0
Medical	1.0
Engineering	6.0
Law Practice	1.0
Social Sciences	1.0
Science	6.0
Others	2.0
	100.0

Table 4.22 represents the occupation of respondents husbands. 25% of them are in Public/Govt. service, 22% are in private service, 6% are self-employed. Tables 4.22 to 4.28 represent the occupational information about the family. Data reveal that 44% of the fathers are in public/government service and 51% mothers are housewives. However, there appears great hesitation about the details of all the relative as non-responsive rate is 45% for husbands, 9% for fathers, 21% for mothers, 48% for sister (1), 94% for sister (2), 55% for brother (1) and 64% for brother (2).

Data on professional status reveals that respondents have not given replies in many cases. However, from the information available it is observed that mothers and sisters professional fields are from social sciences, whereas good number of brothers are from engineering background. This is indicative of the fact that family variables are related with women's professional life.

Table 4.22 discusses the occupation of the husband. 45% didn't reply, 25% are in public/govt. service, 22% are in private service, 6% are self-employed.

TABLE - 4.22
OCCUPATION OF THE HUSBAND

Occupation	*Per cent*
No Reply	45.0
Public/Govt. Service	25.0
Private Service	22.0
Self-employed	6.0
Business	1.0
Others	1.0
	100.0

Table 4.23 gives the occupation of the fathers, 44% are in public/govt. service, 28% are in private service, 4% are self-employed.

TABLE - 4.23
OCCUPATION OF THE FATHER

Occupation	*Per cent*
No reply	9.0
Public/Govt. Service	44.0
Private Service	28.0
Self-employed	4.0
Law	3.0
Research	2.0
Others	10.0
	100.0

Table 4.24 discusses the occupation of the mothers. 51% of the mothers are housewives, 13% are in public/govt. service, 9% are in private service, 6% are in business.

TABLE - 4.24
OCCUPATION OF THE HUSBAND

Occupation	*Per cent*
No reply	21.0
Public/Govt. Service	13.0
Private Service	9.0
Business	6.0
Housewives	51.0
	100.0

Tables 4.25 and 4.26 give the occupation of the sisters. 22% and 3% are housewives, 16% are self-employed, 48% and 94% didn't reply.

TABLE - 4.25
OCCUPATION OF THE SISTER (ONE)

Occupation	*Per cent*
No Reply	48.0
Private Service	3.0
Self-employed	16.0
Business	3.0
Housewives	22.0
Research	4.0
Others	4.0
	100.0

TABLE - 4.26
OCCUPATION OF THE SISTER (TWO)

Occupation	*Per cent*
No Reply	94.0
Public/Govt. Service	2.0
Private Service	1.0
Housewives	3.0
	100.0

Tables 4.27 and 4.28 discuss the occupation of the brothers. Nearly 13% and 3% are in public/government service, 23% and 16% are in private service, 9% and 17% of brothers are in business or self-employed or are in research.

TABLE - 4.27
OCCUPATION OF THE BROTHER (ONE)

Occupation	*Per cent*
No Reply	55.0
Public/Govt. Service	13.0
Private Service	23.0
Self-employed	2.0
Business	5.0
Research	2.0
	100.0

TABLE - 4.28
OCCUPATION OF THE BROTHER (TWO)

Occupation	*Per cent*
No Reply	64.0
Public/Govt. Service	3.0
Private Service	16.0
Self-employed	2.0
Business	7.0
Research	8.0
	100.0

Table 4.29 discusses the annual income of the respondents' parents while they were studying in college. 94% belong to Rs. 50,000/- and above category. Tables 4.29 to 4.46 contain data received in response to questions related to personal information. It is interesting to note that 70% of them are married, 23% of them have arranged marriages, 27% of them are in government services,

59% of them have their own field, where 25% of them have opted for teaching/research. 50% of them have monthly income between 7000-9000, 70% of them have total family income above 17,000, 87% of them have nuclear family and 75% of the respondents have been staying in Delhi for more than 10 years.

TABLE - 4.29
ANNUAL INCOME OF THE RESPONDENTS PARENTS

Group (in Rs.)	*Per cent*
5,000 - 10,000	2.0
10,000 - 20,000	2.0
20,000 - 50,000	2.0
50,000 - and above	94.0
	100.0

Table 4.30 discusses the marital status of the respondents. 70% of the respondents are married and only 22% of them are unmarried.

TABLE - 4.30
MARITAL STATUS OF THE RESPONDENTS

Marital Status	*Per cent*
No Reply	8.0
Married	70.0
Unmarried	22.0
	100.0

Table 4.31 gives the data on type of marriage. 23% of them had arranged marriage, 18% had love marriage and 18% had love-cum-arranged marriage.

TABLE - 4.31
TYPE OF MARRIAGE

Type of Marriage	*Per cent*
No Reply	44.0
Arranged Marriage	23.0
Love Marriage	18.0
Love-cum-Arranged Marriage	15.0
	100.0

Table 4.32 represents the number of children of the respondents. 39% of the respondents didn't reply this question, 32% of the respondents have one child and only 19% have two children.

TABLE - 4.32
NUMBER OF CHILDREN OF THE RESPONDENTS

Children	*Per cent*
No Reply	49.0
1	32.0
2	19.0
	100.0

Table 4.33 gives the picture of educational level of the respondents. Only 28% have done postgraduation. Rest 72% are graduates only.

TABLE - 4.33
EDUCATION OF THE RESPONDENTS

Educational Levels	*Per cent*
Postgraduate	28.0
Graduate	72.0
	100.0

Table 4.34 represents the organizational occupation of the respondents. 11% are in private sector, 27% are in government service, 59% are working in their chosen profession.

TABLE - 4.34
ORGANIZATIONAL OCCUPATION OF THE RESPONDENTS

Occupation	*Per cent*
Private Sector	11.0
Govt. Service	27.0
Professional	59.0
Voluntary Organizations	3.0
	100.0

Table 4.35 suggests that large number of women are working as professionals in their choosen fields, followed by teaching and research jobs. 16% are working in supervisory management level. 25% are in teaching/research, 59% of them are practising professionals.

TABLE - 4.35
TYPE OF JOB OF THE RESPONDENTS

Type	*Per cent*
Supervisory/Managerial	16.0
Teaching/Research	25.0
Professional	59.0
	100.0

Table 4.36 gives a detailed picture of monthly income of the respondents. 50% of the respondents are earning Rs. 7000-9000. 18% are in the income group of Rs. 5000-7000. 15% are between Rs. 9000-11000. Only 12% are earning above Rs. 11,000.

TABLE - 4.36
MONTHLY INCOME OF THE RESPONDENTS

Income Group (in Rs.)	*Per cent*
1000-3000	4.0
3000-5000	1.0
5000-7000	18.0
7000-9000	50.0
9000-11000	15.0
Above 11000	12.0
	100.0

Table 4.37 discusses the total family income of the respondents. 39% of the respondents have family income above Rs. 20,000. 31% are having total family income between Rs. 17000-20000. 18% are having between Rs. 14000-17000. 10% are having between Rs. 11000-14000.

TABLE - 4.37
MONTHLY INCOME OF THE RESPONDENTS

Income Group (in Rs.)	*Per cent*
1000-5000	0.0
5000-8000	1.0
8000-11000	1.0
11000-14000	10.0
14000-17000	18.0
17000-20000	31.0
Above 20000	39.0
	100.0

87% of the respondents live in nuclear families as evident from Table 4.38. Only 11% are living in joint families.

TABLE - 4.38
TYPE OF THE FAMILY OF THE RESPONDENTS

Type	*Per cent*
No Reply	2.0
Nuclear	87.0
Joint	11.0
	100.0

Table 4.39 shows that 70% of the respondents are from North. 12% each are from South and East and only 6% are from Western part of India.

Majority of the respondents are living in Delhi for more than 10 years as evident from Table 4.40, 22% are staying in Delhi for 5-10 years and only 3% are staying in Delhi for less than 5 years.

TABLE - 4.39
PART OF THE COUNTRY RESPONDENTS BELONG TO

Part of India	*Per cent*
North	70.0
South	12.0
West	6.0
East	12.0
	100.0

TABLE - 4.40
RESPONDENTS LIVING IN DELHI

Time period	*Per cent*
Less than 5 years	3.0
5 - 10 years	22.0
Above 10 years	75.0
	100.0

Table 4.41 shows that 90% of the respondents had schooling from city. 10% of them are from town. The academic career of the respondents is presented in Tables 4.41 to 4.54. The data presented shows that 82% of the respondents are from Delhi itself. For 66% the career planning was done at the higher secondary school stage. 22% of them say engineering was their first choice as a career, and parents have been main source of inspiration for 84% of total respondents. 56% of the total have done their post-graduation and only 7% of them have Ph.D to their credit. 53% of the responses say they are not member of association, 57% have excelled in studies holding first rank and while passing out 59% of them were in upper 10-25% category.

TABLE - 4.41
PLACE OF SCHOOLING OF THE RESPONDENTS

Place	*Per cent*
Village	0.0
Town	10.0
City	90.0
	100.0

Table 4.42 discusses the place of education of the respondents. 82% are from Delhi and 18% are from outside Delhi.

TABLE - 4.42
PLACE OF EDUCATION OF THE RESPONDENTS

Place	*Per cent*
Delhi	82.0
Outside Delhi	18.0
	100.0

Table 4.43 represents the medium of instruction of the respondents. 94% are from English medium, 4% are from Hindi medium and rest 2% in other languages.

TABLE - 4.43
MEDIUM OF INSTRUCTION OF THE RESPONDENTS

Medium of Instruction	*Per cent*
English	94.0
Hindi	4.0
Other	2.0
	100.0

Table 4.44 discusses the types of schools of the respondents. 51% are from public schools. 19% are from Kendriya Vidyalayas, 15% are from Christian Missionary, 11% are from Government/ Semi-Government schools.

TABLE - 4.44
TYPE OF SCHOOL OF THE RESPONDENTS

Type	*Per cent*
Public	51.0
Kendriya Vidyalaya	19.0
Christian Missionary	15.0
Govt./Semi-Govt.	11.0
Others	4.0
	100.0

Table 4.45 discusses the nature of the school of the respondents. 76% are from coeducational background. 22% are from purely girls school.

TABLE - 4.45
NATURE OF THE SCHOOL OF THE RESPONDENTS

Nature of School	*Per cent*
All girls	22.0
Coeducational	76.0
No Reply	2.0
	100.0

Table 4.46 gives the data about the planning of the career by the respondents. 24% of them planned their career at secondary school stage, 66% of them planned at higher secondary school level, 10% never planned their career.

TABLE - 4.46
PLANNING OF CAREER BY THE RESPONDENTS

Level	*Per cent*
Secondary School Stage	24.0
Higher Secondary School Stage	66.0
Never Planned	10.0
	100.0

Table 4.47 gives the data about present career as a first choice of the respondents. For 22% of the respondents, it was their first choice and for 66% of the respondents, it was not their first choice.

TABLE - 4.47
PRESENT CAREER AS A FIRST CHOICE OF THE RESPONDENTS

Choice	*Per cent*
No Reply	12.0
Yes	22.0
No	66.0
	100.0

Table 4.48 discusses the individual's influence on respondent's choice. 47% of them say that it was their mother's influence, but for 37% of the respondents, it was their father who played an important role in their choice.

TABLE - 4.48
INDIVIDUAL'S INFLUENCE ON RESPONDENTS CHOICE

Relative	*Per cent*
Mother	47.0
Father	37.0
Science Teacher	3.0
Brother	1.0
College Contacts	1.0
Others	11.0
	100.0

Table 4.49 gives us a picture about respondents. 37% of them are graduate engineers but only 56% are postgraduates. Only 7% of them have done their Ph.D.

TABLE - 4.49
EDUCATIONAL QUALIFICATION OF WOMEN ENGINEERS

Educational Level	*Per cent*
Graduates	37.0
Postgraduates	56.0
Ph.D.	7.0
	100.0

Table 4.50 discusses membership of association held by respondents. Only 39% of them are members of association and 53% are not members of the association.

TABLE - 4.50
MEMBER OF ASSOCIATION

Reply	*Per cent*
No Reply	8.0
Yes	39.0
No	53.0
	100.0

Table 4.51 shows the rank in the school of the respondents, 57% come in upper 10% category, 32% of them come in the upper 10-25% category and 11% come in the 25-50% category.

TABLE - 4.51
RESPONDENTS RANK IN SCHOOL

Group	*Per cent*
In the Upper 10%	57.0
In the Upper 10-25%	32.0
In the Upper 25-50%	11.0
	100.0

Table 4.52 gives the data on the approximate rank of the respondents in their class. 26% stood in the upper 10% category, 59% come in 10-25% category and only 9% come in 25-50% category.

TABLE - 4.52
APPROXIMATE RANK OF THE RESPONDENTS

Group	*Per cent*
No Reply	6.0
Upper 10%	26.0
10-25%	59.0
25-50%	9.0
	100.0

Perception of Self

Tables 4.53 and 4.54 present the self-perception of the respondents in terms of their personal drive and determination, self-confidence and intellectual abilities. The study reveals that only 27% of the women consider themselves having high personal drive and determination, whereas 68% of them think that they have high degree of self-confidence and 40% perceive themselves as high in intellectual abilities.

Table 4.53 gives data about perception of personal drive and determination. For 13% it is low. 57% respondents feel it is average and 27% feel it is high.

TABLE - 4.53
PERCEPTION OF PERSONAL DRIVE DETERMINATION

Level	*Per cent*
No Reply	3.0
Low	13.0
Average	57.0
High	27.0
	100.0

Table 4.54 shows level of self-confidence. 5% feel it is low. For 27% it is average and 68% respondents have high level of self-confidence.

TABLE - 4.54
LEVEL OF SELF-CONFIDENCE

Level	*Per. cent*
Low	5.0
Average	27.0
High	68.0
	100.0

Table 4.55 gives data about respondents intellectual abilities. For 4% it is low. But 56% of the respondents feel it is average whereas 40% of the respondents feel their intellectual ability is quite high.

TABLE - 4.55
INTELLECTUAL ABILITIES

Level	*Per cent*
Low	4.0
Average	56.0
High	40.0
	100.0

Occupational Choices and Patterns

Tables 4.56 to 4.67 present the occupational choices and patterns. It can be seen that 71% of them had specific preference to the type of job at the time of graduation. Those who wanted either desk type job or executive are 27% and 43% respectively. For 72% of them the preference for job hasn't changed. 39% of them are working as Industrial Entrepreneur, 15% of them as research scientists, 27% of them as consultants. For 75% of the respondents there have been no breaks in career. 17% who had breaks in career, were either due to marriage or pregnancy. Poor response was evident from the data when asked about reasons for fulfilment. 88% did not reply this question. 37% of them say they have never refused a job. However, for 85% of the respondents their present job does fulfil their expectations.

Table 4.56 represents the job at the time of graduation. 71% of the respondents feel they had the choice at that time. For 25% it was no choice.

TABLE - 4.56
JOB OF THE RESPONDENTS AT THE TIME OF GRADUATION

Reply	*Per cent*
No reply	4.0
Yes	71.0
No	25.0
	100.0

Table 4.57 represents the type of jobs of the respondents. 27% of the respondents have desk type job, 43% are performing executive jobs, 25% of the respondents performing marketing and management type of job.

TABLE - 4.57
TYPE OF JOB OF THE RESPONDENTS

Type	*Per cent*
Desk Type Job	27.0
Executive	43.0
Marketing and Management	28.0
Any Other	2.0
	100.0

Table 4.58 represents the data on change of preference of work. 21% of the respondents says yes. But 72% of the respondents feel their preference for work has not changed.

TABLE - 4.58
PREFERENCE IN CHANGE OF WORK

Reply	*Per cent*
No Reply	7.0
Yes	21.0
No	72.0
	100.0

Table 4.59 gives the data about current professional status. 15% of the respondents are in research, 6% are Executive, 39% are in industries, 10% are employed consultant and 17% are self-employed consultants.

TABLE 4.59
CURRENT PROFESSIONAL STATUS

Profession	*Per cent*
Practising Professional	4.0
Research Scientist	15.0
Executive/Manager	6.0
Industrial/Entrepreneur	39.0
Academic Research Teacher	2.0
Consultant (Employee)	10.0
Consultant (Self-employed)	17.0
Any Other	7.0
	100.0

Table 4.60 gives the data about field of specialization and first job respondents had. For 99% of the respondents it was in the same field of specialization.

TABLE - 4.60
FIELD OF SPECIALIZATION AND THE 1ST JOB

Reply	*Per cent*
Yes	99.0
No	1.0
	100.0

Table 4.61 discusses nature of present job. 29% are in teaching, 59% are in R & D, 1% are in design and 10% are in production.

TABLE - 4.61
NATURE OF PRESENT JOB

Nature of Present Job	*Per cent*
No Reply	0.0
Teaching	29.0
Research & Development	59.0
Design	1.0
Production	10.0
Consultant	1.0
	100.0

Table 4.62 discusses specific nature of work of the respondents. 9% of the respondents are in policy development. 8% are in production, planning, execution, 12 are in supervision of production and 44% are in specialized area.

TABLE - 4.62
SPECIFIC NATURE OF WORK OF THE RESPONDENTS

Nature of Work	*Per cent*
No Reply	4.0
Policy Development	9.0
Production Planning/Execution	8.0
Supervision of Production	12.0
Testing	17.0
Documentation	6.0
Specialized Area	44.0
	100.0

Table 4.63 gives data on current management responsibility held by the respondents. 11% are in top level, 68% are in the middle level of management and 15% are in lower level of management.

TABLE - 4.63
CURRENT MANAGEMENT RESPONSIBILITY HELD BY THE RESPONDENTS

Level	*Per cent*
No Reply	6.0
Top Level	11.0
Middle Level	68.0
Lower Level	15.0
	100.0

Table 4.64 discusses breaks in career of the respondents. 17% of the respondents had break in their career whereas 75% didn't have any break in their career.

TABLE - 4.64
BREAKS IN CAREER OF THE RESPONDENTS

Reply	*Per cent*
No Reply	8.0
Yes	17.0
No	75.0
	100.0

Table 4.65 gives the data on refusal of a job by the respondents. 58% of the respondents say yes but 37% of the respondents say no.

TABLE - 4.65
REFUSAL OF A JOB BY THE RESPONDENTS

Reply	*Per cent*
No Reply	5.0
Yes	58.0
No	37.0
	100.0

Table 4.66 discusses expectations of the respondents. 85% of the respondents say yes and 13% of the respondents say no.

TABLE - 4.66
WHETHER EXPECTATIONS OF THE RESPONDENTS FULFILLED

Reply	*Per cent*
No Reply	2.0
Yes	85.0
No	13.0
	100.0

Table 4.67 gives the reasons for fulfilment of expectations and aspirations. Very poor response was evident as 88% did not respond.

TABLE - 4.67
REASONS FOR FULFILMENT OF EXPECTATIONS

Reason	*Per cent*
No Reply	88.0
Sound Financial Status	1.0
Better Working Environment	6.0
Part Time	1.0
Challenging	4.0
	100.0

Quality of Work Life

Table 4.68 gives the attitude of the management towards respondents. The attitude of the management has been based on merit and quality concept and is preferred by 54% of the respondents and for 28% of the respondents it is fair and just. 68% of the respondents say that any lapse on their part is being counselled. Their relationship with their colleagues have been cooperative and concerned for majority of them (65%). 48% of them give all the reasons when asked about attitude towards their subordinates. 10% say that the attitude is firm and official, 26% human and concern for well-being and 14% participative. Satisfaction is the main factor for the present job is felt by 40% of the respondents, followed by job suited to their qualifications (23%).

Table 4.68 discusses the data on attitude of the management towards respondents. 28% of the respondents find it fair and just, 54% find that merit and quality are given due recognition, only 5% of the respondents see different treatment to male/female counterparts.

TABLE - 4.68
ATTITUDE OF THE MANAGEMENT TOWARDS RESPONDENTS

Attitude	*Per cent*
No Reply	8.0
Fair and Just	28.0
Merit and Quality Recognized	54.0
Different Treatment to Male/ Female Counterpart	5.0
Not Fair	5.0
	100.0

Table 4.69 gives data on lapse on the part of respondents. 24% didn't reply but 68% find it is being counselled.

TABLE - 4.69
LAPSE ON THE PART OF RESPONDENTS

Attitude	*Per cent*
No Reply	24.0
Admonished	7.0
Counselled	68.0
Ignored	1.0
	100.0

Table 4.70 discusses the data on relationship with subordinates. 65% find it cooperative and concerned and 33% cordial and friendly.

TABLE - 4.70
RELATIONSHIP WITH SUBORDINATES

Attitude	*Per cent*
No Reply	2.0
Cordeal and Friendly	33.0
Cooperative and Concerned	65.0
	100.0

Table 4.71 gives the data on respondents attitude towards subordinates. 48% of them say it is combination of all the three factors, where 10% say it is firm and official. 26% say it is humane and concerned for their well-being and 14% say it is participative and consultative.

TABLE - 4.71
ATTITUDE TOWARDS SUBORDINATES

Attitude	*Per cent*
No Reply	2.0
Firm and Official	10.0
Humane and Concerned for their well-being	26.0
Participative and Consultative	14.0
All Three, Depending upon the Situation	48.0
	100.0

Table 4.72 gives the data on factors that influenced respondents decision for the present job. 23% say it is best suited to their qualification and 40% say satisfaction is the basic factors for the present job.

TABLE - 4.72
FACTORS THAT INFLUENCE DECISION ABOUT THE PRESENT JOB

Factor	*Per cent*
Suited to my Qualification	23.0
Forced Circumstances	8.0
Satisfaction	40.0
Friend's/Neighbour's/Relation's/Influence	2.0
Doing a Job is the in Thing	2.0
Sound Job	1.0
Job has Promotion Avenues	5.0
Social Status	5.0
Any Other	14.0
	100.0

Socio-cultural Attitude

Tables 4.73 to 4.78 give information about attitudes. 100% of the women feel that woman as a mother has great responsibility towards rearing children. But 75% of the respondents also feel that three months maternity leave is not adequate for the working women. 100% of them agree that absence of working mother for number of hours does have negative effect on the development of children. 62% of the respondents feel that as a working person only sometimes they are able to meet with the social commitments and obligations.

Table 4.73 discusses the data on responsibility of a mother. It is very interesting that 100% of the women agree to it.

TABLE - 4.73

WHETHER A WOMAN HAS RESPONSIBILITIES AS A MOTHER

Reply	*Per cent*
Yes	100.0
	100.0

Table 4.74 gives the data on facilities for children at the place of work and society in general. 82% of them said it doesn't provide but 8% say sometimes and 6% say yes.

TABLE - 4.74

FACILITIES FOR CHILDREN AT THE PLACE OF WORK AND SOCIETY IN GENERAL

Reply	*Per cent*
No Reply	4.0
Yes	6.0
Sometimes	8.0
No	82.0
	100.0

Table 4.75 gives the respondents views on three months maternity leave. 25% of them are satisfied with it but 75% say it is not enough and should be extended to a longer period.

TABLE - 4.75

WHETHER THREE MONTHS MATERNITY LEAVE IS ENOUGH

Reply	*Per cent*
Yes	25.0
No	75.0
	100.0

Tables 4.76 to 4.78 give the respondents view on mothers effect on children. 100% of them agree that it does.

TABLE - 4.76
WORKING MOTHERS' EFFECT ON THEIR CHILDREN

Effect on Children	*Per cent*
Yes	100.0
	100.0

TABLE - 4.77
NEGATIVE IMPACT OF WORKING MOTHER

Negative Impact	*Per cent*
Health	1.0
Emotional Development	18.0
Mental Development	13.0
Performance in the Class	1.0
All/Some of Above	67.0
	100.0

TABLE - 4.78
POSITIVE IMPACT OF WORKING MOTHER ON HER CHILDREN

Positive Impact	*Per cent*
Becomes Independent	2.0
Taking up Responsibility	10.0
More Sensible and Matured	15.0
Any Other	1.0
All/Some of Above	72.0
	100.0

Table 4.79 gives respondents view on social commitment and obligation. 62% say they sometimes fulfil them, only 35% do fulfil and only 3% say no to this question.

TABLE - 4.79
FULFILLING SOCIAL COMMITMENTS AND OBLIGATIONS

View	*Per cent*
Yes	35.0
No	3.0
Sometimes	62.0
	100.0

Domestic Information

In Tables 4.80 to 4.87 the data presented discuss the domestic information of the respondents. The married respondents did feel a change in division of work in the house. But 99% are not happy with the existing division of labour in an Indian society and 100% of them feel that they should have a say in the decision making. When asked about giving a choice they did like to opt for any other type of career 39% said yes and 57% said no. 47% of the respondents say that present career is of their own choice and 33% feel that parents have been major influence in selecting their present career.

Table 4.80 gives respondents feeling about change in division of household work. 42% find a positive change. 54% find it sometimes and 4% find no change at all.

TABLE - 4.80
CHANGE IN DIVISION OF WORK (IN THE HOUSE)

Reply	*Per cent*
Yes	42.0
Sometimes	54.0
No	4.0
	100.0

Table 4.81 gives respondents views on help by spouse in domestic work. 64% of the respondents didn't reply. 27% say that their spouses don't help them at all.

TABLE - 4.81
DOMESTIC WORK—HELP BY SPOUSE

Reply	*Per cent*
No Reply	64.0
Yes	8.0
No	28.0
	100.0

Table 4.82 gives respondents views about division of labour in the household. 99% of them show their dissatisfaction.

TABLE - 4.82
SATISFACTION WITH DIVISION OF LABOUR IN THE HOUSEHOLD

Satisfaction	*Per cent*
Yes	1.0
No	99.0
	100.0

Tables 4.83 and 4.84 give data on decision-making in the family. 100% of them agree that women should have a say in the decision making and 94% of them felt that they should have a say in more than one area.

TABLE - 4.83
DECISION MAKING IN THE FAMILY

Should women have a say	*Per cent*
Yes	100.0
	100.0

TABLE - 4.84
AREAS OF DECISION MAKING

Area	*Per cent*
Expenditure and Family Budget	1.0
Marriage of Children	4.0
General Household Decision	1.0
More than one	94.0
	100.0

Table 4.85 discusses respondents views on given a choice would they like to have a different career. 57% don't want to have a different career but 39% want to change. Only 4% of them were not sure.

TABLE - 4.85
GIVEN A CHOICE WILL THEY LIKE TO HAVE A DIFFERENT CAREER

Reply	*Per cent*
No Reply	4.0
Yes	39.0
No	57.0
	100.0

Table 4.86 discusses the data on influence in career of the respondents. 47% say it is their own choice, but 33% give credit to their parents, 17% of them say any other person.

TABLE - 4.86
INFLUENCE IN CAREER OF THE RESPONDENTS

Relative	*Per cent*
Parents	33.0
Brother/Sister	2.0
Your Own Choice	47.0
Teacher	1.0
Any Other Person	17.0
	100.0

99% of the respondents have said that they are not satisfied with the division of work in the household. Similarly all the engineer women participants of this study feel that women should have a say in decision making which include areas such as family budget, future of children, and general household decisions.

As discussed before parents do influence the career choice of these women, yet 47% have said that career is their own choice. This also suggest that need for achievement and competence are present in significant level. One of the surprising facts that emerges from this study of women engineers is that teachers are supposed to be great advisers so far as the choice of career is concerned. But in this case only one per cent of the respondents feel so.

The study reveals that 85% of the total respondents were of the view that intercaste marriages are better whereas 15% felt that intercaste marriages are for the worst. The reason for increase in divorce rate was due to adjustment problems was felt by 53% of the women followed by changing position of the women not easily acceptable.

TABLE - 4.87
VIEWS ON INTERCASTE MARRIAGES

View	*Per cent*
Better	85.0
Worst	15.0
	100.0

Table 4.88 gives respondents views on reasons for increase in divorce rate in the country. 53% find it is because of adjustment problems. 28% say it is because of changing position of women not easily acceptable. Self-awareness of women is increasing in the view of 11% of the respondents, 5% say it is age of marriage and 3% say it is because women are becoming increasingly economically independent.

TABLE - 4.88
REASONS FOR INCREASE IN DIVORCE RATE

Reason	*Per cent*
Economically Independent	3.0
Self-awareness of Women is Increasing	11.0
Age of Marriage	5.0
Adjustment Problems	53.0
Changing Position of Women not Easily Acceptable	28.0
	100.0

Work Psychology

Tables 4.89 to 4.96 deal with respondents view on aspects of work psychology. Aspects of work psychology deal with satisfaction, values, performance, frustration and preferences. 31% of the respondents perceive work with total life psychology and feel work is meaning of life, followed by better utilization of time for 20% of the respondents. Surprising fact in the context of today's changing values is that only 5% of them have said that they work for earning money and enjoyment.

TABLE - 4.89
REASONS FOR WORKING

Reason	*Per cent*
Livelihood	4.0
Earn Money and Enjoy Life	5.0
Better Utilization of Time	20.0
Meaning of Life	31.0
Better Opportunities for Spending Time	20.0
Desire to do Something	1.0
Any Other	19.0
	100.0

TABLE - 4.90
SELF EVALUATION OF THEIR WORK

Self-evaluation	*Per cent*
Not a Good Job Performer	9.0
Average Job Performer	6.0
Good Job Performer	62.0
Excellent Job Performer	23.0
	100.0

Self-evaluation of work suggests that 62% of the respondents perceive themselves as good job performers and 23% as excellent job performers. Only 9% feel that they are not good performers. This reveals that in the working there is high degree of work motivation.

Tables 4.91 to 4.96 further focus mainly on work psychology. 53% give happy family life, as a reason for satisfaction in personal life as compared to 35% giving emphasis on the career development. Involvement in creative activities was the primary source of satisfaction in professional lives was felt by 44% of the respondents. Parental attitude was responsible for the low representation of women in engineering was felt by 45% of the respondents. 57% of the women feel that a job in this profession is demanding in nature. 63% of them did favour this field as profession and advised to take up this career.

Table 4.91 discusses respondents views on factors contributing to satisfaction in personal life. 53% say it is happy family life and 35% contribute to career development.

TABLE - 4.91
FACTORS CONTRIBUTING TO SATISFACTION IN PERSONAL LIFE

Factor	*Per cent*
Career Development	35.0
Help to the Husband	1.0
Happy Family Life	53.0
Growth Development of the Children	5.0
Any Other	6.0
	100.0

Table 4.92 gives respondents views about satisfaction in professional life. 44% say it is intellectual stimulation. For 24% it is exposure to new techniques and 12% say it is because of financial advancement and 16% say that it involves them in creative activities.

TABLE - 4.92
SATISFACTION IN PROFESSIONAL LIFE

View	*Per cent*
No Reply	2.0
Exposure to New Technique	24.0
Opportunity to Help the Country	1.0
Financial Advancement	12.0
Involvement in Creative Activities	16.0
Intellectual Stimulation	44.0
Any Other	1.0
	100.0

Parental discouragement and tough competition was seen as main reason for low representation of women in professional colleges as is evident from Table 4.93.

TABLE - 4.93
REASONS FOR LOW REPRESENTATION OF WOMEN

Perception of women	*Per cent*
No Reply	6.0
Parental Discouragement	45.0
Engineering Skills	1.0
Teacher's Attitude	2.0
Non-acceptability of Women Engineers	19.0
Boys are More Intelligent than Girls	1.0
Any Other (like Tough Competitions)	26.0
	100.0

Table 4.94 discusses the reasons for low representation of women in profession. For 57% it is that women want to work only part time. 17% each find male resentment and business community's attitude responsible for it.

TABLE - 4.94
LOW REPRESENTATION IN THE PROFESSION

Reason	*Per cent*
No Reply	9.0
Women want to Work only Part Time	57.0
Men in this Field Resent Women Colleagues	17.0
Business Community will never accept Women Engineers	17.0
	100.0

Table 4.95 gives preference of the respondents for superiors/subordinates. 61% of this do not have any preference. Only 6% preferred women and 14% men as their subordinates/senior.

TABLE - 4.95
PREFERENCE OF THE RESPONDENTS

Reply	*Per cent*
No Reply	19.0
Would Prefer a Woman	6.0
Would Prefer a Man	14.0
No Preference	61.0
	100.0

Table 4.96 gives respondents advice on taking up their career. 63% say with certainty to take up their career. 22% say no and 15% say yes for the field.

TABLE - 4.96
ADVICE BY THE RESPONDENTS

Reply	*Per cent*
Qualified No	22.0
Qualified Yes	15.0
Most Certainly	63.0
	100.0

Study reveals that parents are major source of discouragement to girls wanting to take up engineering profession as the per cent was as high as 45%.

Women Architects of Delhi

Tables 4.97 to 4.110 present personal/background variables of the architects majority of the women are between the age group of 25-30 years. 40% of the total respondents belong to small family consisting of an only child. 60% of them belong to family having two or more children. 50% of the respondents have only one brother and 22% of the respondents have one sister. 60% of the respondents' mothers are graduates and 38% are postgraduates whereas 54% of the fathers are postgraduates. The respondents who are married have an equally qualified husband and in-laws family. 32% of the respondents' husbands are postgraduates.

Personal Information of the Respondents

Table 4.97 gives information about the age of the respondents. 2% of the respondents are less than 25 years. 88% of them are between the age group of 25-30 years and 10% are above the age of 30 years.

TABLE - 4.97
AGE OF THE RESPONDENTS

Age Group	*Per cent*
Below 25 years	2.0
25-30 years	88.0
31 and above	10.0
	100.0

Table 4.98 gives data on birth order of the respondents. 40% belong to only one child category. 20% are the eldest child in the family. 20% are middle child in the family.

TABLE - 4.98
BIRTH ORDER OF THE RESPONDENTS

Birth Order	*Per cent*
Only Child	40.0
Eldest Child	20.0
Middle Child	20.0
Any Other	20.0
	100.0

Tables 4.99 and 4.100 give information about the number of brothers and sisters of the respondents. 42% don't have any brother and 66% don't have any sister. 50% and 22% have one brother and one sister. Only 8% have more than one brother and 6% have more than one sister. 4% have three sisters and 2% have four sisters.

TABLE - 4.99
NUMBER OF BROTHERS OF THE RESPONDENTS

Number	*Per cent*
0	42.0
1	50.0
2	8.0
3	0.0
	100.0

TABLE - 4.100
NUMBER OF SISTERS OF THE RESPONDENTS

Number	*Per cent*
0	66.0
1	22.0
2	6.0
3	4.0
4	2.0
	100.0

Table 4.101 shows that 2% of mothers of the respondents have high school education. 60% of them are graduates and 38% are postgraduates.

TABLE - 4.101
MOTHERS' EDUCATION OF THE RESPONDENTS

Educational Level	*Per cent*
High School	2.0
Graduate	60.0
Postgraduate	38.0
	100.0

Table 4.102 shows the educational level of the fathers. 20% of fathers of the respondents have passed high school. 26% of them are graduates and 54% are postgraduates.

TABLE - 4.102
FATHERS' EDUCATION OF THE RESPONDENTS

Educational Level	*Per cent*
High School	20.0
Graduate	26.0
Postgraduate	54.0
	100.0

Tables 4.103 and 4.104 show the educational level of the sisters of the respondents. 16% of the sisters are graduates and 34% are postgraduates. 50% and 86% didn't reply back.

TABLE - 4.103
EDUCATION OF THE RESPONDENTS' SISTER (ONE)

Educational Level	*Per cent*
No Reply	50.0
Graduate	16.0
Postgraduate	34.0
	100.0

TABLE - 4.104
EDUCATION OF THE RESPONDENTS' SISTER (TWO)

Educational Level	*Per cent*
No Reply	86.0
High School	00.0
Graduate	14.0
	100.0

Tables 4.105 and 4.106 show the educational level of brothers. 46% and 90% didn't reply as they belong to small family. 16% and 6% are graduates respectively. 32% and 4% are postgraduates.

TABLE - 4.105
EDUCATION OF RESPONDENTS' BROTHER (ONE)

Educational Level	*Per cent*
No Reply	46.0
High School	6.0
Graduate	16.0
Postgraduate	32.0
	100.0

TABLE - 4.106
EDUCATION OF RESPONDENTS' BROTHER (TWO)

Educational Level	*Per cent*
No Reply	90.0
Graduate	6.0
Postgraduate	4.0
	100.0

Table 4.107 shows the educational level of the husbands. 60% didn't reply at all. 8% of them are graduates and 32% are postgraduates.

TABLE - 4.107
EDUCATION OF THE RESPONDENTS' HUSBANDS

Educational Level	*Per cent*
No Reply	60.0
Graduate	8.0
Postgraduate	32.0
	100.0

Table 4.108 gives respondents' mother-in-laws education. 60% didn't reply back. 6% have lower school 14% have high school education, 14% are graduates and 6% are postgraduates.

TABLE - 4.108
RESPONDENTS' MOTHER-IN-LAWS EDUCATION

Educational Level	*Per cent*
No Reply	60.0
Lower School	6.0
High School	14.0
Graduate	14.0
Postgraduate	6.0
	100.0

Father-in-laws education is shown in Table 4.109. 60% didn't reply at all, 4% have done high school, 28% are graduates and 8% are postgraduates.

TABLE - 4.109
RESPONDENTS' FATHER-IN-LAWS EDUCATION

Educational Level	*Per cent*
No Reply	60.0
High School	4.0
Graduate	28.0
Postgraduate	8.0
	100.0

Profession and Occupation of Parents and Relations

The data presented in Tables 4.110 to 4.123 give the detailed picture of profession and occupation chosen by the family members. Majority of the married respondents have their life partners from engineering background (14%) whereas 40% fathers are from engineering background, 18% and 10% of the spouses are working in public or private sector. In case of respondents, fathers are working in public/private organizations with 54% in public/government organizations and 38% in private organizations respectively. 80% of the mothers are housewives.

Table 4.110 gives husbands' profession. 56% didn't reply. 2% are from medical background, 14% are from engineering background, 2% are from teaching, 8% are law graduates and 18% belong to different profession.

TABLE - 4.110
HUSBANDS' PROFESSION

Profession	*Per cent*
No Reply	56.0
Medical	2.0
Engineering	14.0
Teaching	2.0
Law Graduates	8.0
Others	18.0
	100.0

Table 4.111 shows fathers' profession. 8% didn't reply. 4% of them are from agricultural background, 20% are from medical

background, 40% are from engineering background, 12% are from law and 10% are from teaching and 6% are from different profession.

TABLE - 4.111
FATHERS' PROFESSION

Profession	*Per cent*
No Reply	8.0
Agriculture	4.0
Medical	20.0
Engineering	40.0
Law Practice	12.0
Teaching	10.0
Others	6.0
	100.0

Table 4.112 gives mothers' profession. 34% didn't reply. 52% belong to teaching profession, 8% are from medical and 6% are from other professions.

TABLE - 4.112
MOTHERS' PROFESSION

Profession	*Per cent*
No Reply	34.0
Medical	8.0
Teaching	52.0
Others	6.0
	100.0

Tables 4.113 and 4.114 give sisters' profession. 64% and 92% didn't reply. 18% are from medical, 8% from teaching and 4% from research and 6% from other professions.

TABLE - 4.113
SISTERS' PROFESSION (ONE)

Profession	*Per cent*
No Reply	64.0
Medical	18.0
Teaching	8.0
Research	4.0
Others	6.0
	100.0

TABLE - 4.114
SISTERS' PROFESSION (TWO)

Profession	*Per cent*
No Reply	92.0
Teaching	8.0
	100.0

Tables 4.115 and 4.116 show the profession of the brothers. 46% and 94% didn't answer. 14% are from medical, 34% from engineering and 6% are from different professions.

TABLE - 4.115
BROTHERS' PROFESSION (ONE)

Profession	*Per cent*
No Reply	46.0
Medical	14.0
Engineering	34.0
Others	6.0
	100.0

TABLE - 4.116
BROTHERS' PROFESSION (TWO)

Profession	*Per cent*
No Reply	94.0
Research	6.0
	100.0

Table 4.117 gives data on husbands' occupation. 58% didn't reply. 18% are from public sector, 10% are from private sector, 6% are self-employed and 8% from other professions.

TABLE - 4.117
HUSBANDS' OCCUPATION

Occupation	*Per cent*
No Reply	58.0
Public/Government Sector	18.0
Private Sector	10.0
Self-employed	6.0
Others	8.0
	100.0

Table 4.118 shows fathers' occupation. 4% give no reply. 54% are from public/government service, 38% from private service and 4% from different professions.

TABLE - 4.118
FATHER'S OCCUPATION

Occupation	*Per cent*
No Reply	4.0
Public/Govt. Service	54.0
Private Service	38.0
Others	4.0
	100.0

Table 4.119 gives mothers' occupation. 14% of the mothers are working in public/govt. service, 4% are from private service, 2% are from business, 80% are housewives.

TABLE - 4.119
MOTHERS' OCCUPATION

Occupation	*Per cent*
Public/Govt. Service	14.0
Private Service	4.0
Business	2.0
Housewife	80.0
	100.0

Tables 4.120 and 4.121 give data on respondents' sisters occupation. Poor response is evident. 68% and 92% didn't reply. 8% and 1% are in public/government service, 14% and 1% are in private jobs.

TABLE - 4.120
SISTERS' OCCUPATION (ONE)

Occupation	*Per cent*
No Reply	68.0
Public/Govt. Service	8.0
Private Service	14.0
Business	6.0
Housewife	2.0
	2.0
	100.0

TABLE - 4.121
SISTERS' OCCUPATION (TWO)

Occupation	*Per cent*
No Reply	92.0
Public/Govt. Service	1.0
Private Service	1.0
Self-employed	2.0
Housewife	4.0
	100.0

Tables 4.122 and 4.123 give details on respondents' brothers occupation. 45% and 90% didn't give any details, 14% and 15% are in public/government service, 31% and 2% are in private jobs and 2% and 3% are in different occupations.

TABLE - 4.122
BROTHERS' OCCUPATION (ONE)

Occupation	*Per cent*
No Reply	45.0
Public/Govt. Service	14.0
Private Service	31.0
Business	5.0
Research	3.0
Others	2.0
	100.0

TABLE - 4.123
BROTHERS' OCCUPATION (TWO)

Occupation	*Per cent*
No Reply	90.0
Public/Govt. Service	5.0
Private Service	2.0
Others	3.0
	100.0

Personal Status of the Respondents

Tables 4.124 to 4.135 present the data on personal background of the respondents. 96% of them are from high income background, 60% of the respondents are unmarried and remaining 40% of them are married and 64% of them have only one child. 36% of them are earning Rs. 7000 to 9000 per month, 56% of the respondents having family income Rs. 20,000. 96% are from Northern part of the country and 96% of them have stayed in Delhi for above 10 years.

Table 4.127 gives annual income of the respondents' parental income. 25 didn't reply, 2% had annual income of Rs. 20,000 to 50,000 per annum. 96% come in Rs. 50,000 and above category.

TABLE - 4.124
ANNUAL INCOME OF THE RESPONDENTS' PARENTS

Income Group (in Rs.)	*Per cent*
No Reply	2.0
20,000-50,000	2.0
50,000 and above	96.0
	100.0

Table 4.125 shows that 40% of the respondents are married and 60% are unmarried.

TABLE - 4.125
MARITAL STATUS OF THE RESPONDENTS

Marital Status	*Per cent*
Married	40.0
Unmarried	60.0
	100.0

Table 4.126 shows that 60% respondents didn't reply when asked which type of marriage they had. 22% had arranged one, 6% love marriage and 12% love-cum-arranged marriage.

TABLE - 4.126
TYPE OF MARRIAGE OF THE RESPONDENTS

Type of Marriage	*Per cent*
No Reply	60.0
Arranged	22.0
Love Marriage	6.0
Love-cum-Arranged Marriage	12.0
	100.0

Table 4.127 shows number of children respondents had. 64% had one child, 20% had two children, 16% didn't have any child.

TABLE - 4.127
NUMBER OF CHILDREN OF THE RESPONDENTS

No. of Children	*Per cent*
One Child	64.0
Two Children	20.0
No Child	16.0
	100.0

Table 4.128 shows that 5% of the respondents are post-graduates and 95% are graduates.

TABLE - 4.128
EDUCATIONAL QUALIFICATION OF THE RESPONDENTS

Educational Qualification	*Per cent*
Postgraduation	5.0
Graduation	95.0
	100.0

Table 4.129 shows the Organizational occupation of the respondents. 2% are in business, 4% are in private service, 14% are in government service and 80% are professionals.

TABLE - 4.129
ORGANIZATIONAL OCCUPATION OF THE RESPONDENTS

Occupation	*Per cent*
Business	2.0
Private Service	4.0
Government Service	14.0
Professional	80.0
	100.0

Table 4.130 shows nature of job held by the respondents. 8% are either in teaching or research and 92% are practising their own professions.

TABLE - 4.130
NATURE OF JOB

Nature of Job	*Per cent*
Teaching/Research	8.0
Professionals	92.0
	100.0

Table 4.131 gives information about the respondents monthly income. 6% fall in first group, 26% comes in second group, 36% come in third group, 28% in fourth group and only 4% in the fifth group of above Rs. 11,000.

TABLE - 4.131
MONTHLY INCOME OF THE RESPONDENTS

Income Group (in Rs.)	*Per cent*
3000-5000	6.0
5000-7000	26.0
7000-9000	36.0
9000-11000	28.0
Above 11000	4.0
	100.0

Table 4.132 shows the total family income of the respondents. 6% are in first category, 10% come in second category, 28% in the third category and 56% in the fourth category of above Rs. 20,000.

TABLE - 4.132
TOTAL FAMILY INCOME OF THE RESPONDENTS

Income Group (in Rs.)	*Per cent*
11000-14000	6.0
14000-17000	10.0
17000-20000	28.0
Above 20000	56.0
	100.0

Table 4.133 shows that 96% of the respondents live in nuclear families and 4% live in joint families.

TABLE - 4.133

TYPE OF FAMILY OF THE RESPONDENTS

Type of the Family	*Per cent*
Nuclear	96.0
Joint	4.0
	100.0

Table 4.134 gives information about part of the country respondents belong. 96% are from north, 2% each from south and west and no one from east.

TABLE - 4.134

PART OF THE COUNTRY RESPONDENTS BELONG TO

Part of the Country	*Per cent*
North	96.0
South	2.0
West	2.0
East	0.0
	100.0

Table 4.135 gives information about respondents stay in Delhi. 2% have been staying for below 5 years, 2% are in Delhi for 5-10 years and 96% are in Delhi for above 10 years.

TABLE - 4.135

STAY IN DELHI BY RESPONDENTS

Time Period	*Per cent*
Below 5 Years	2.0
5-10 Years	2.0
Above 10 Years	96.0
	100.0

Academic Life of the Respondents

Tables 4.136 to 4.150 represent the data regarding the academic career of the respondents. 94% of them have been brought up in cities and 70% are from Delhi itself. 100% of the respondents had English as a medium of instruction. 40% of them are from public schools, with 56% of the women from coeducational background, 62% of them planned their career at higher secondary level. For 64% of them say present career is their first choice. For 74% of the respondents, parents had influenced and supported in their choice of career. Only 40% of them have done their post-graduation in their field. 92% of the respondents are members of the association. 96% of them have been in the above 25% in the class ranks having fared better than rest of them in their profession. Most of them have average personal qualities when asked about self-perception.

TABLE - 4.136
PLACE OF SCHOOLING OF THE RESPONDENTS

Place of Schooling	*Per cent*
Village	0.0
Town	6.0
City	94.0
	100.0

Table 4.137 shows 70% of the respondents are from Delhi and only 30% are from outside Delhi.

TABLE - 4.137
STATE OF THE RESPONDENTS

State	*Per cent*
Delhi	70.0
Outside Delhi	30.0
	100.0

TABLE - 4.138
MEDIUM OF INSTRUCTION OF THE RESPONDENTS

Medium	*Per cent*
English	100.0
	100.0

Table 4.139 shows 40% of the respondents had schooling from public schools, 30% each from Kendriya Vidyalaya and Christian Missionary schools.

TABLE - 4.139
TYPE OF SCHOOL OF THE RESPONDENTS

Type of School	*Per cent*
Public School	40.0
Kendriya Vidyalaya	30.0
Christian Missionary	30.0
	100.0

TABLE - 4.140
NATURE OF SCHOOL OF THE RESPONDENTS

Nature of School	*Per cent*
All Girls School	44.0
Coeducational School	56.0
	100.0

Table 4.141 gives information that 62% planned their career at higher school level, 36% at secondary school level and 2% never planned their career.

TABLE - 4.141
PLANNING OF CAREER BY THE RESPONDENTS

Level	*Per cent*
Secondary School	36.0
Higher School	62.0
Never Planned	2.0
	100.0

Table 4.142 shows that for 64% of the respondents' present career was their first choice and 34% say 'no' when asked about their views about their present career.

TABLE - 4.142
PRESENT CAREER OF THE RESPONDENTS

Reply	*Per cent*
No Reply	2.0
Yes	64.0
No	34.0
	100.0

Table 4.143 shows that parents have been main source of inspiration in selecting career, 10% brothers and sisters and for 16% it has been influence of relatives, teachers and friends.

TABLE - 4.143
INDIVIDUAL INFLUENCE IN RESPONDENTS CHOICE

Source of Inspiration	*Per cent*
Mother	34.0
Father	40.0
Brother/Sister	10.0
Others	16.0
	100.0

TABLE - 4.144
EDUCATIONAL QUALIFICATION OF ARCHITECTS

Educational Qualification	*Per cent*
Graduates	60.0
Postgraduates	40.0
	100.0

Table 4.145 shows that 92% of the respondents are members of an association and 8% are not.

TABLE - 4.145
MEMBER OF AN ASSOCIATION

Reply	*Per cent*
No Reply	4.0
Yes	92.0
No	4.0
	100.0

Table 4.146 shows that 48% of the respondents come in the upper 10% and 48% of the respondents in the 10-25% category and 2% in the 25-50% category.

TABLE - 4.146
RANK IN THE CLASS OF THE RESPONDENTS

Reply	*Per cent*
No Reply	2.0
Upper 10%	48.0
10-25%	48.0
25-50%	2.0
	100.0

TABLE - 4.147
APPROXIMATE RANK OF THE RESPONDENTS

Category	*Per cent*
No Reply	2.0
Upper 10%	40.0
10-25%	50.0
25-50%	2.0
	100.0

Perception of Self

Tables 4.148 to 4.150 show perception of self, 40% have high personal drive and determination, 68% have high self-confidence and 40% have high intellectual abilities.

TABLE - 4.148
PERSONAL DRIVE AND DETERMINATION

Level	*Per cent*
Low Average	2.0
Average	58.0
High	40.0
	100.0

TABLE - 4.149
SELF-CONFIDENCE IN THE RESPONDENTS

Level	*Per cent*
Low Average	2.0
Average	30.0
High	68.0
	100.0

TABLE - 4.150
INTELLECTUAL ABILITIES OF THE RESPONDENTS

Level	*Per cent*
Low Average	2.0
Average	58.0
High	40.0
	100.0

Occupational Patterns

Tables 4.151 to 4.166 discuss the occupational patterns of the respondents. 78% of the respondents knew the type of job they wanted to have after graduation. For 68% of the respondents, the preference remains the same, with 64% of them working as professionals, 29% of the respondents are into designing. 30% of the respondents are into middle level management. 36% of the women maintain that there is no break in their career. For 18% of the women break in their career is because of marriage and pregnancy. 54% of them find merit and quality performance is given due recognition and any lapse on their part is counselled for 68%. Their relationship with subordinates is cooperative and concerned for 52% of them. It is felt by majority of the respondents that the main factor which influenced their decision for the present job is that the job was suited for their qualification.

Table 4.151 gives information that 78% of the respondents knew the type of job they wanted at the time of graduation, but 20% showed their ignorance.

TABLE - 4.151
SPECIFIC REFERENCE TO JOB BY THE RESPONDENTS AT THE TIME OF GRADUATION

Reply	*Per cent*
No Reply	2.0
Yes	78.0
No	20.0
	100.0

Table 4.152 gives the respondents' view about type of the job they wanted. 24% of them didn't reply. 52% are doing desk job, 12% are executives, 8% are in marketing and management.

TABLE - 4.152
TYPE OF JOB

Type	*Per cent*
No Reply	24.0
Desk Job	52.0
Executive	12.0
Marketing and Management	8.0
Any Other	4.0
	100.0

Table 4.153 shows the respondents' change of preferences of work. 30% said 'yes' when asked about it and 68% said 'no' when asked about their change of preference of work.

TABLE - 4.153

CHANGE OF PREFERENCE FOR /OF WORK BY THE RESPONDENTS

Reply	*Per cent*
No Reply	2.0
Yes	30.0
No	68.0
	100.0

Table 4.154 gives data regarding current professional status of the respondents. 64% are practising professionals, 6% are in research, 14% are consultant and 10% are in others.

TABLE - 4.154

CURRENT PROFESSIONAL STATUS OF THE RESPONDENTS

Reply	*Per cent*
No Reply	2.0
Practising Professional	64.0
Executive/Manager	4.0
Academic Researcher	6.0
Consultant	14.0
Any Other	10.0
	100.0

TABLE - 4.155

FIELD OF SPECIALIZATION AND FIRST JOB

Reply	*Per cent*
No Reply	4.0
Yes	92.0
No	4.0
	100.0

Table 4.156 gives the data on nature of present job of women architects. 4% are in designing, 6% are in production, 46% are in consultancy, 2% are specialists and 20% are doing any other job.

TABLE - 4.156
NATURE OF PRESENT JOB OF WOMEN ARCHITECTS

Nature of Job	*Per cent*
Designing	4.0
Production	6.0
Construction	2.0
Consultancy	46.0
Specialist	2.0
Consultant	18.0
Project Planning	2.0
Any Other	20.0
	100.0

Table 4.157 presents data regarding specific nature of job of the respondents. 12% didn't reply, 12% are in policy development, 12% are in planning, 12% are in execution, 11% in supervision, 29% are in designing.

TABLE - 4.157
SPECIFIC NATURE OF WORK OF THE RESPONDENTS

Nature of Job	*Per cent*
No Reply	12.0
Policy Development	12.0
Documentation	12.0
Planning	12.0
Execution	12.0
Supervision	11.0
Designing	29.0
	100.0

TABLE - 4.158
CURRENT MANAGEMENT RESPONSIBILITY OF THE RESPONDENTS

Level	*Per cent*
No Reply	44.0
Lower Level	22.0
Middle Level	30.0
High Level	4.0
	100.0

Table 4.159 gives data about breaks in career. 46% didn't reply. 18% said 'yes' and 36% said 'no'.

TABLE - 4.159
BREAKS IN CAREER OF THE RESPONDENTS

Reply	*Per cent*
No Reply	46.0
Yes	18.0
No	36.0
	100.0

TABLE - 4.160
REFUSAL OF A JOB BY THE RESPONDENTS

Reply	*Per cent*
No Reply	10.0
Yes	50.0
No	40.0
	100.0

TABLE - 4.161
EXPECTATIONS OF THE RESPONDENTS ABOUT THE JOB

Reply	*Per cent*
No Reply	8.0
Yes	70.0
No	22.0
	100.0

Table 4.162 presents data about attitude of the management towards respondents. 15% didn't reply. 28% feel that it is fair and just, 54% feel that merit and quality is given due recognition, 2% feel different treatment to male/female counterpart and 1% are not fair.

TABLE - 4.162
ATTITUDE OF THE MANAGEMENT TOWARDS THE RESPONDENTS

Reply	*Per cent*
No Reply	15.0
Fair and Just	28.0
Merit and Quality given due Recognition	54.0
Different Treatment to Male/Female Counterpart	2.0
Not Fair	1.0
	100.0

Table 4.163 presents the data on lapse on the part of respondents. 15% didn't reply, 15% agree it is being admonished, 68% feel counselled and 2% feel it is ignored.

Table 4.163
LAPSES ON THE PART OF THE RESPONDENTS

Reply	*Per cent*
No Reply	15.0
Admonished	15.0
Counselled	68.0
Ignored	2.0
	100.0

Table 4.164 presents the data about respondents' relationship with subordinates. 6% feel it is indifferent, 42% say it is cordial and friendly and 52% finds it cooperative and concerned.

TABLE - 4.164
RELATIONSHIP WITH SUBORDINATES

Attitude	*Per cent*
Indifferent	6.0
Cordial and Friendly	42.0
Cooperative and Concerned	52.0
	100.0

Table 4.165 presents the data on respondents' attitude towards subordinates. 2% say it is firm and official. 20% feel it is humane and concerned, 28% feel it is authoritative and consultative and 50% feel it is all the above three.

TABLE - 4.165
ATTITUDE TOWARDS SUBORDINATES

Attitude	*Per cent*
Firm and Official	2.0
Humane and Concerned	20.0
Authoritative and Consultative	28.0
All Three Depending upon the Situation	50.0
	100.0

TABLE - 4.166
FACTORS THAT INFLUENCED DECISION OF RESPONDENTS FOR THE PRESENT JOB

Influencing Factor	*Per cent*
No Reply	4.0
Suited to the Qualification	39.0
Circumstances	4.0
Satisfaction	17.0
Relative's Influence	2.0
Doing a Job is "In Thing"	2.0
Financially Sound	10.0
Promotional Avenues	10.0
Social Status	2.0
Utilize the Time in Productive Way	10.0
	100.0

Socio-cultural Information

Information is presented in Tables 4.167 to 4.173. 90% of the women feel that as a mother they have great responsibilities. 66% feel that neither society nor organizations provide any facilities. For majority of the respondents 76% feel that three months maternity leave is not enough and feel it should be six months to one year. 98% of the respondents feel working mothers have effect on the development of children. 40% of the architects feel as working person they are able to meet the social commitments and obligations.

TABLE - 4.167
RESPONSIBILITIES OF WOMEN AS A MOTHER

Reply	*Per cent*
Yes	90.0
No	8.0
No Reply	2.0
	100.0

Table 4.168 discusses about facilities provided by organizations and society. 4% didn't reply, 10% said 'yes', 20% feel sometimes and 66% said 'no' when asked about it.

TABLE - 4.168
FACILITIES PROVIDED BY ORGANIZATIONS AND SOCIETY

Reply	*Per cent*
No Reply	4.0
Yes	10.0
Sometimes	20.0
No	66.0
	100.0

TABLE - 4.169
WHETHER THREE MONTHS MATERNITY LEAVE IS ENOUGH

Reply	*Per cent*
No Reply	4.0
Yes	20.0
No	76.0
	100.0

Table 4.170 presents data on working mothers' effect on their children. 98% feel it does have an impact on children.

TABLE - 4.170
WORKING MOTHERS' EFFECT ON CHILDREN

Effect on Children	*Per cent*
No Reply	2.0
Yes	98.0
	100.0

Table 4.171 presents data on negative impact of working mother. 4% didn't reply, 6% feel it is on health, 31% on emotional development, 6% feel it is on mental development, 4% feel on the performance, 45% feel it is all/some of above.

TABLE - 4.171
NEGATIVE IMPACT OF WORKING MOTHER

Negative Impact	*Per cent*
No Reply	4.0
Health	6.0
Emotional Development	31.0
Mental Development	6.0
Performance in the Class	4.0
Shyness	4.0
All/Some of Above	45.0
	100.0

Table 4.172 presents data on positive impact of working mother. 6% didn't reply, 13% feel children become independent, 7% feel it makes them more responsible, 2% find it makes them extrovert and 51% find it is all/some of the above.

TABLE - 4.172
POSITIVE IMPACT OF WORKING MOTHER

Positive Impact	*Per cent*
No Reply	6.0
Becomes Independent	13.0
Taking up Responsibility	7.0
More Sensible and Mature	21.0
Extrovert	2.0
All/Some of the Above	51.0
	100.0

Table 4.173 presents data on social commitments and obligation. 8% didn't reply, 40% said 'yes' they fulfil their obligation and commitments, 4% said 'no' and 48% felt that they 'sometimes' fulfil their commitments and obligation.

TABLE - 4.173
SOCIAL COMMITMENTS AND OBLIGATION

Reply	*Per cent*
No Reply	8.0
Yes	40.0
No	4.0
Sometimes	48.0
	100.0

Domestic Information

Tables 4.174 to 4.179 present domestic informations. 50% feel there has been a change in division of work between husband and wife in the house. 100% of the respondents feel that they should have a say in the decision making in all the areas. 77% of them don't want to have a different career. Mainly parents have influenced them to have architecture as a profession.

Table 4.174 presents data on domestic life of the respondents. 2% didn't reply, 50% feel 'yes', 23% feel 'sometimes' and 25% feel there is 'no' change in it.

TABLE - 4.174
DOMESTIC LIFE OF THE RESPONDENTS (DIVISION OF WORK IN THE HOUSE)

Change	*Per cent*
No Reply	2.0
Yes	50.0
Sometimes	23.0
No	25.0
	100.0

TABLE - 4.175 .
DIVISION OF LABOUR IN INDIAN SOCIETY

Reply	*Per cent*
Yes	0.0
No	100.0
	100.0

Table 4.176 presents respondents' views on decision making in the family. 100% feel that women should have a say in family.

TABLE - 4.176
DECISION MAKING IN THE FAMILY

Reply	*Per cent*
Yes	100.0
	100.0

Table 4.177 shows that 100% of respondents feel women should have a say in all the areas.

TABLE 4.177
WOMEN SHOULD HAVE A SAY IN ALL THE AREAS

Reply	*Per cent*
All the Areas	100.0
	100.0

Table 4.178 gives data on respondents' views on would they have a different career. 2% of the respondents didn't reply, 21% said 'yes' and 77% said 'no'.

TABLE - 4.178
GIVEN A CHOICE WOULD YOU HAVE A DIFFERENT CAREER

Reply	*Per cent*
No Reply	2.0
Yes	21.0
No	77.0
	100.0

TABLE - 4.179
INFLUENCE IN CAREER CHOICE

Influencing Factor	*Per cent*
Parents	50.0
Brother/Sister	2.0
Own Choice	40.0
Teachers	2.0
Any Other	6.0
	100.0

Tables 4.180 to 4.183 give their views on Intercaste marriage and reasons for increase in divorce rate. 85% of the respondents feel intercaste marriages are better. Only 13% of them feel that it is not good. 46% of the respondents attribute adjustment problems for increase in divorce rate in the country. Whereas 31% of the architects feel that changing position of the women is not easily acceptable in the society. Better utilization of time 23%, better opportunities 23% were the important reasons for their work. Almost 51% of them consider themselves as good job performers and 25% consider themselves to be excellent job performers.

TABLE - 4.180
VIEWS ON INTERCASTE MARRIAGE

Reply	*Per cent*
Yes	85.0
No	13.0
No Reply	2.0
	100.0

Table 4.181 presents data on reasons for increase in divorce rate. 4% feel it is because they are becoming economically independent, 15% feel because self-awareness among women is increasing, 46% feel it is because of adjustment problems and 31% feel changing position of women is not easily acceptable.

TABLE - 4.181
REASONS FOR INCREASE IN DIVORCE RATE

Reason	*Per cent*
Economically Independence	4.0
Self-awareness of Women on the Rise	15.0
Age of Marriage	4.0
Adjustment Problem	46.0
Changing Position of Women not Easily Acceptable	31.0
	100.0

Table 4.182 presents respondents' views on their preference for work. 13% want to earn money and enjoy life, 23% for better utilization of time, for 10% it is meaning of life, 23% are working because of better opportunity and 21% are working because of desire to do something.

TABLE - 4.182
PREFERENCE FOR WORK OF THE RESPONDENTS

Reason	*Per cent*
Earn Money and Enjoy Life	13.0
Better Utilization of Time	23.0
Meaning of Life	20.0
Better Opportunity	23.0
Desire to do Something	21.0
	100.0

TABLE - 4.183
SELF-EVALUATION OF THE RESPONDENTS CAREER

Comment	*Per cent*
Not a Good Job Performer	16.0
Average Job Performer	8.0
Good Job Performer	51.0
Excellent Job Performer	25.0
	100.0

Work Psychology

Data is presented in Tables 4.184 to 4.190. Career development is the primary source of satisfaction for 60% of the respondents. Exposure to new techniques is the primary source of satisfaction for 12% of the respondents. Tough competition (32%) was seen as a main reason for low representation. 39% of them feel that the job is too demanding and women wish to work part time. It is very interesting to note that 72% of the respondents have no preference as far as choice of superior or subordinates are concerned. 50% of the women feel one should take up this field and 15% of respondents feel the attitude of the teachers discouraging.

TABLE - 4.184
PRIMARY SOURCE OF INSPIRATION IN PERSONAL LIFE

Reason	*Per cent*
Career Development	60.0
Help to the Husband	8.0
Happy Family Life	21.0
Growth and Development of Children	4.0
Any Other	7.0
	100.0

Table 4.185 gives data on inspiration in respondents' professional life. 41% didn't reply. For 12% it is exposure to new techniques, for 10% it is opportunity to help the country, financial development for 29%, and it is an involvement in creative activities for 8%.

TABLE - 4.185
INSPIRATION IN PROFESSIONAL LIFE OF THE RESPONDENTS

Reason	*Per cent*
No Reply	41.0
Exposure to New Techniques	12.0
Opportunity to Help the Country	10.0
Financial Advancement	29.0
Involvement in Creative Activities	8.0
	100.0

TABLE - 4.186
REASONS FOR LOW REPRESENTATION OF WOMEN (QUALIFICATION)

Reason	*Per cent*
No Reply	33.0
Parental Discouragement	4.0
Engineering Skill	10.0
Teacher's Attitude	15.0
Non-acceptability of Women in the Field	6.0
Tough Competition	32.0
	100.0

TABLE - 4.187
REASONS FOR LOW REPRESENTATION (IN PROFESSIONAL LIFE)

Reason	*Per cent*
No Reply	2.0
Desire to Work Part Time	39.0
Men's Resentment	16.0
Business Community Attitude	9.0
Working Environment	16.0
Any Other	18.0
	100.0

Table 4.188 gives respondents' views on preference of the respondents (for superiors). 6% respondents preferred women whereas 22% preferred men and 72% did not show any preference.

TABLE - 4.188
PREFERENCE OF THE RESPONDENTS (FOR SUPERIORS)

Choice	*Per cent*
Women	6.0
Men	22.0
No Preference	72.0
	100.0

Table 4.189 gives respondents' preference for subordinates. 2% didn't reply, 7% would prefer a woman, 19% would prefer a man and 72% didn't show any preference.

TABLE - 4.189
PREFERENCE OF THE RESPONDENTS (FOR SUBORDINATES)

Reply	*Per cent*
No Reply	2.0
Would Prefer a Woman	7.0
Would Prefer a Man	19.0
No Preference	72.0
	100.0

Table 4.190 gives respondents' advise to others. 50% of them feel people should have their career most certainly, 43% say 'yes', 2% said 'no' and 5% say emphatically no.

TABLE - 4.190
ADVISE BY THE RESPONDENTS

Reply	*Per cent*
Most Certainly	50.0
Yes	43.0
No	2.0
Emphatic No.	5.0
	100.0

Women Doctors of Delhi

Background Variable

The age distribution, birth order and family background of the respondents is presented in Table 4.191. Personal information of each of them is given. It is seen that the percentage of women above 30 is 30% as compared to 70% in the age group of below 30. Most of them belong to small families having not more than one brother or sister. Most of them belong to families which are highly qualified in which parents are either graduates or postgraduates. Respondents who are married have their spouses from equally highly qualified backgrounds.

Table 4.191 presents the age of the respondents. 44% of them are below 25 years. 26% are in the age group of 25-30 years and rest 30% are in the age group of 30 and above.

TABLE - 4.191
AGE OF THE RESPONDENTS

Group	*Per cent*
Below 25 Years	44.0
25-30 Years	26.0
30 and Above	30.0
	100.0

Table 4.192 gives the birth order of the respondents. 31% are in the only child category, 23% of them are eldest, 20% of them are in middle child category, 23% are in the last child category.

TABLE - 4.192
BIRTH ORDER OF THE RESPONDENTS

Birth Order	*Per cent*
Only Child	31.0
Eldest Child	23.0
Middle Child	20.0
Last Child	23.0
Any Other	3.0
	100.0

Tables 4.193 and 4.194 give the education of the parents. 47% of the fathers and 18% of the mothers are postgraduates, 27% of the fathers and 21% of the mothers are graduates, 18% of the fathers and 49% of the mothers are high school and 8% of the fathers and 12% of the mothers have lower school education.

TABLE - 4.193
EDUCATION OF THE RESPONDENTS' FATHERS

Educational Level	*Per cent*
Postgraduate	47.0
Graduate	27.0
High School	18.0
Lower School	8.0
	100.0

TABLE - 4.194
EDUCATION OF THE RESPONDENTS' MOTHERS

Educational Level	*Per cent*
Postgraduate	18.0
Graduate	21.0
High School	49.0
Lower School	12.0
	100.0

TABLE - 4.195
EDUCATION OF THE RESPONDENTS' SISTERS (ONE)

Educational Level	*Per cent*
Postgraduate	2.0
Graduate	8.0
High School	48.0
Lower School	42.0
	100.0

TABLE - 4.196
EDUCATION OF THE RESPONDENTS' SISTERS (TWO)

Educational Level	*Per cent*
Postgraduate	52.0
Graduate	6.0
High School	18.0
Lower School	24.0
	100.0

Tables 4.197 and 4.198 give the data on the education of the brothers. 55% and 34% of them are postgraduates, 25% and 32% are graduates, 15% and 33% are in high school, 5% and 1% are in lower school.

TABLE - 4.197
EDUCATION OF THE RESPONDENTS' BROTHERS (ONE)

Educational Level	*Per cent*
Postgraduate	55.0
Graduate	25.0
High School	15.0
Lower School	5.0
	100.0

TABLE - 4.198
EDUCATION OF THE RESPONDENTS' BROTHERS (TWO)

Educational Level	*Per cent*
Postgraduate	34.0
Graduate	32.0
High School	33.0
Lower School	1.0
	100.0

Table 4.199 gives the education of respondents' husbands. 53% did not reply. 37% of them are postgraduates, 10% of them are graduates.

TABLE - 4.199
EDUCATION OF THE RESPONDENTS' HUSBANDS

Educational Level	*Per cent*
No Reply	53.0
Postgraduate	37.0
Graduate	10.0
High School	00.0
Lower School	00.0
	100.0

Table 4.200 gives the educational level of respondents' mother-in-laws. 52% didn't reply, 5% are postgraduates, 17% of them are graduates, 16% are high school and 10% are lower school.

TABLE - 4.200
EDUCATION OF THE RESPONDENTS' MOTHER IN-LAWS

Educational Level	*Per cent*
No Reply	52.0
Postgraduate	5.0
Graduate	17.0
High School	16.0
Lower School	10.0
	100.0

Table 4.201 presents the educational level of father-in-laws of the respondents. 56% didn't reply, 4% are postgraduates, 18% are graduates, 17% are high school and 5% are lower school.

TABLE - 4.201
EDUCATION OF THE RESPONDENTS' FATHER IN-LAWS

Educational Level	*Per cent*
No Reply	56.0
Postgraduate	4.0
Graduate	18.0
High School	17.0
Lower School	5.0
	100.0

Professional and Occupational Background

Tables 4.202 and 4.203 present the data on the professional background and occupation of the respondents and their families. 29% of them have husbands from medical profession. Brothers and sisters are also with professional background. 78% of the respondents' fathers and 42% of husbands are either working with private organizations or government organizations. Very few are doing their own business or practice 9% in case of spouses and 17% in the case of fathers. 67% of the mothers of the respondents are housewives.

Table 4.202 gives the profession of the respondents' husbands. 3% are in agriculture, 57% are in medical, 26% are in engineering, 13% are in law practice and 1% are in teaching.

TABLE - 4.202
PROFESSION OF THE RESPONDENTS' HUSBANDS

Profession	*Per cent*
Agriculture	3.0
Medical	57.0
Engineering	26.0
Law Practice	13.0
Teaching	1.0
	100.0

TABLE - 4.203
PROFESSION OF THE RESPONDENTS' FATHERS

Profession	*Per cent*
No Reply	52.0
Medical	29.0
Engineering	7.0
Law Practice	5.0
Teaching	7.0
	100.0

Table 4.204 presents the profession of the respondents' mothers. 68% didn't reply, 13% are in medical, 3% are in engineering, 12% are in law practice and 4% are in teaching.

TABLE - 4.204
PROFESSION OF THE RESPONDENTS' MOTHERS

Profession	*Per cent*
No Reply	68.0
Agriculture	0.0
Medical	13.0
Engineering	3.0
Law Practice	12.0
Teaching	4.0
	100.0

TABLE - 4.205
PROFESSION OF THE RESPONDENTS' SISTERS (ONE)

Profession	*Per cent*
No Reply	62.0
Medical	13.0
Engineering	13.0
Law Practice	6.0
Teaching	6.0
	100.0

TABLE - 4.206
PROFESSION OF THE RESPONDENTS' SISTERS (TWO)

Profession	*Per cent*
No Reply	47.0
Agriculture	2.0
Medical	19.0
Engineering	22.0
Teaching	2.0
Social Sciences	3.0
Science	1.0
Others	4.0
	100.0

Tables 4.207 and 4.208 give the profession of the brothers. 50% and 53% did not reply, 1% and 5% are in agriculture, 15% and 14% are in medical, 28% and 25% are in engineering and 6% and 3% are in other professions.

TABLE - 4.207
PROFESSION OF THE RESPONDENTS' BROTHERS (ONE)

Profession	*Per cent*
No Reply	50.0
Agriculture	1.0
Medical	15.0
Engineering	28.0
Others	6.0
	100.0

TABLE - 4.208
PROFESSION OF THE RESPONDENTS' BROTHERS (TWO)

Profession	*Per cent*
No Reply	53.0
Agriculture	5.0
Medical	14.0
Engineering	25.0
Others	3.0
	100.0

Table 4.209 presents the data on occupation of the husbands of the respondents. 46% didn't reply, 16% are in public/government

service, 26% are in private service, 5% are self-employed, 4% are in business and 3% are in other professions.

TABLE - 4.209
OCCUPATION OF THE RESPONDENTS' HUSBANDS

Occupation	*Per cent*
No Reply	46.0
Public/Government Service	16.0
Private Service	26.0
Self-employed	5.0
Business	4.0
Others	3.0
	100.0

TABLE - 4.210
OCCUPATION OF THE RESPONDENTS' FATHERS

Occupation	*Per cent*
Public/Government Service	60.0
Private Service	18.0
Self-employed	7.0
Business	10.0
Others	5.0
	100.0

Table 4.211 presents the data on the occupation of mothers of the respondents. 2% did not reply, 22% are in public/govt. service, 5% are in private service, 1% are self-employed, 3% are in business and 67% are housewives.

TABLE - 4.211
OCCUPATION OF THE RESPONDENTS' MOTHERS

Occupation	*Per cent*
No Reply	2.0
Public/Government Service	22.0
Private Service	5.0
Self-employed	1.0
Business	3.0
Housewife	67.0
	100.0

TABLE - 4.212
OCCUPATION OF THE RESPONDENTS' SISTER (ONE)

Occupation	*Per cent*
No Reply	00.0
Public/Government Service	53.0
Private Service	22.0
Self-employed	7.0
Business	4.0
Housewife	14.0
	100.0

TABLE - 4.213
OCCUPATION OF THE RESPONDENTS' SISTER (TWO)

Occupation	*Per cent*
No Reply	3.0
Public/Government Service	63.0
Private Service	17.0
Self-employed	2.0
Business	11.0
Housewife	4.0
	100.0

Table 4.214 presents the occupation of the brothers. 11% did not reply, 32% are in public/govt. service, 32% are in private service, 9% are self-employed, 14% are in business and 2% are in other categories.

TABLE - 4.214
OCCUPATION OF THE RESPONDENTS' BROTHER (ONE)

Occupation	*Per cent*
No Reply	11.0
Public/Government Service	32.0
Private Service	32.0
Self-employed	9.0
Business	14.0
Others	2.0
	100.0

Table 4.215 gives the occupation of the brothers of the respondents (two). 46% didn't reply, 11% are in public/government

service, 20% are in private service, 3% are self-employed, 7% are in business, 4% are in research and 9% are in other categories.

TABLE - 4.215
OCCUPATION OF THE RESPONDENTS' BROTHER (TWO)

Occupation	*Per cent*
No Reply	46.0
Public/Government Service	11.0
Private Service	20.0
Self-employed	3.0
Business	7.0
Research	4.0
Others	9.0
	100.0

Personal Information

Tables 4.216 and 4.217 contain data about the personal information about the respondents. 77% of them have annual income of Rs. 50,000 and above, it is interesting to note that 46% of them have love or love-cum-arranged marriages and 47% of them have small children in the age group of below 5 years.

As far as educational background is concerned, 94% of them have ticked the option profession. 88% of them are working in their own fields and 6% are in government service. 53% of them have monthly income between Rs. 5000-7000. 32% of them have total family income above Rs. 20,000. 82% of them belong to nuclear families and 68% of the respondents are from northern part of India. 42% of the total respondents have been staying in Delhi for more than 10 years.

TABLE - 4.216
ANNUAL INCOME OF THE RESPONDENTS' PARENTS AT THE TIME OF STUDIES

Group	*Per cent*
No Reply	11.0
5,000-10,000	7.0
10,000-20,000	1.0
20,000-50,000	4.0
50,000 and above	77.0
	100.0

Table 4.217 presents the data on marital status of the respondents. 5% didn't reply, 53% are married, 41% are unmarried and 1% are widows.

TABLE - 4.217
MARITAL STATUS OF THE RESPONDENTS

Marital Status	*Per cent*
No Reply	5.0
Married	53.0
Unmarried	41.0
Widow	1.0
	100.0

Table 4.218 presents the data on different types of marriages. 53% have arranged marriage, 31% have love marriage, 15% have love-cum-arranged marriage and 1% had any other type of marriage.

TABLE - 4.218
TYPE OF MARRIAGE

Type	*Per cent*
Arranged Marriage	53.0
Love Marriage	31.0
Love-cum-Arranged Marriage	15.0
Any Other	1.0
	100.0

TABLE - 4.219
NUMBER OF CHILDREN

Age Group	*Per cent*
0-5 Years	47.0
5-10 Years	20.0
10-15 Years	31.0
Above 15 Years	2.0
	100.0

TABLE - 4.220
EDUCATIONAL QUALIFICATION

Educational Level	*Per cent*
Graduate	1.0
Postgraduate	5.0
Professional	94.0
	100.0

Table 4.221 gives the details about organizations in which respondents are working. 1% are working in private sector, 16% are in government sector and 83% are working as practising professionals.

TABLE - 4.221
TYPE OF ORGANIZATIONS

Type	*Per cent*
Private Sector	1.0
Government Sector	16.0
Practising Professionals	83.0
	100.0

Table 4.222 presents the data about nature of job. 6% are in administration, 88% are in their own professions, 3% are in research, 2% are self-employed and 1% are in voluntary organizations.

TABLE - 4.222
NATURE OF JOB OF THE RESPONDENTS

Nature of Job	*Per cent*
Administration	6.0
Profession	88.0
Research	3.0
Self-employed	2.0
Voluntary Organizations	1.0
	100.0

TABLE - 4.223
MONTHLY INCOME OF THE RESPONDENTS

Income Group (in Rs.)	*Per cent*
5,000 - 7,000	53.0
7,000 - 9,000	24.0
9,000 - 11,000	16.0
Above 11,000	7.0
	100.0

Table 4.224 gives the total family income of the respondents. 2% didn't reply, 2% are in the second category, 19% are in the third

category, 24% are in the fourth category, 10% are in the fifth category, 11% are in the sixth category and 32% are in the seventh category.

TABLE - 4.224
TOTAL FAMILY INCOME

Income Group (in Rs.)	*Per cent*
No Reply	2.0
5,000-8,000	2.0
8,000-11,000	19.0
11,000-14,000	24.0
14,000-17,000	10.0
17,000-20,000	11.0
Above 20,000	32.0
	100.0

Table 4.225 presents the data on family type. 2% didn't reply, 82% are staying in nuclear family and 10% belong to joint family.

TABLE - 4.225
FAMILY TYPE

Type of Family	*Per cent*
No Reply	2.0
Nuclear	82.0
Joint	16.0
	100.0

TABLE - 4.226
PART OF THE COUNTRY

Part of India	*Per cent*
No Reply	6.0
North	68.0
South	16.0
North East	1.0
West	8.0
East	1.0
	100.0

Table 4.227 gives the data about their stay in Delhi, 47% are staying in Delhi for less than 5 years, 11% are staying for 5-10 years and 42% are staying in Delhi for above 10 years.

TABLE - 4.227
STAY IN DELHI

Time Period	*Per cent*
Less than 5 Years	47.0
5-10 Years	11.0
Above 10 Years	42.0
	100.0

Academic Career

The academic career of the respondents is presented in Tables 4.228 and 4.229. The data presented here show 57% of them have schooling in cities. 69% of them are from Delhi itself. For 91% of them the medium of instruction was English. 52% of them are from public schools. 73% of them are from girls schools. For 56% the career planning was done at higher secondary school stage. 57% of them have their first choice as a career and parents have been the main source of inspiration for 63% of total respondents. 81% of the total have done their postgraduation; no one has Ph.D to their credit. 62% of the responses say that they are members of association and while passing out 50% of them were in second category of upper 10-25%. Personal qualities in the achievement of academic goals have been either average or high.

Table 4.228 presents the data on place of schooling. 15% had their schooling in villages, 28% had in towns and 57% had in cities.

TABLE - 4.228
PLACE OF SCHOOLING

Place	*Per cent*
Village	15.0
Town	28.0
City	57.0
	100.0

Table 4.229 gives the data on states where their schooling took place. 2% didn't reply, 29% had schooling outside Delhi and 69% had it in Delhi.

TABLE - 4.229
STATE WHERE SCHOOLING TOOK PLACE

Place	*Per cent*
No Reply	2.0
Outside Delhi	29.0
Delhi	69.0
	100.0

TABLE - 4.230
ACADEMIC CAREER — TYPE OF SCHOOL

Type of School	*Per cent*
No Reply	2.0
Public	52.0
Kendriya Vidyalaya	17.0
Christian Missionary	10.0
Government/Semi-Government	4.0
Municipal	2.0
Private	13.0
	100.0

TABLE - 4.231
MEDIUM OF INSTRUCTION

Medium	*Per cent*
No Reply	2.0
Other Languages	7.0
English	91.0
	100.0

Table 4.232 presents the data on planning of career by the respondents. 2% didn't reply, 36% did the planning at secondary school level, 56% at higher secondary level and 6% never planned.

TABLE - 4.232
PLANNING OF CAREER BY THE RESPONDENTS

Career Planning	*Per cent*
No Reply	2.0
Secondary	36.0
Higher Secondary	56.0
Never Planned	6.0
	100.0

Table 4.233 gives the data on type of school. 73% had their schooling in all girls school and 27% had coeducational schooling.

TABLE - 4.233
TYPE OF SCHOOL

Type	*Per cent*
All Girls	73.0
Coeducational	27.0
	100.0

TABLE - 4.234
PRESENT CAREER AS FIRST CHOICE

Reply	*Per cent*
No Reply	9.0
Yes	57.0
No	34.0
	100.0

TABLE - 4.235
INFLUENCE OF RELATIVES IN THE CHOICE OF PROFESSION

Relative	*Per cent*
No Reply	25.0
Mother	23.0
Father	40.0
Maths Teacher	4.0
Science Teacher	4.0
Sister	2.0
Others	2.0
	100.0

Table 4.236 presents the data on educational qualification of women doctors. 19% are graduates and 81% are postgraduates.

TABLE - 4.236
EDUCATIONAL QUALIFICATION OF WOMEN DOCTORS

Educational Level	*Per cent*
Graduates	19.0
Postgraduates	81.0
Ph.D.	0.0
	100.0

Table 4.237 gives the data on respondents being member of association. 4% didn't reply, 62% are members and 34% aren't members of any association.

TABLE - 4.237
MEMBERSHIP OF ASSOCIATION

Reply	*Per cent*
No Reply	4.0
Yes	62.0
No	34.0
	100.0

TABLE - 4.238
RANKING IN SCHOOL

Category	*Per cent*
No Reply	24.0
In the Upper 10-25%	49.0
In the Upper 25-50%	27.0
	100.0

Table 4.239 gives the approximate rank while passing out of the college. 18% come in the first category, 50% are in upper 10-25% category and 32% are in the third category.

TABLE - 4.239
APPROXIMATE RANKING WHILE PASSING OUT OF THE COLLEGE

Category	*Per cent*
Upper 10%	18.0
Upper 10-25%	50.0
Upper 25-50%	32.0
	100.0

Tables 4.240 to 4.242 give their views about self-perception. 40%, 46% and 53% had average and 55%, 44% and 22% have high self-perception, self-confidence and intellectual abilities.

TABLE - 4.240
SELF-PERCEPTION, PERSONAL DRIVE AND DETERMINATION TO ACHIEVE

Level	*Per cent*
Low	5.0
Average	40.0
High	55.0
	100.0

TABLE - 4.241
SELF-CONFIDENCE

Levels	*Per cent*
Low	10.0
Average	46.0
High	44.0
	100.0

TABLE - 4.242
INTELLECTUAL ABILITIES

Levels	*Per cent*
Low	25.0
Average	53.0
High	22.0
	100.0

Occupational Patterns

From Tables 4.243 to 4.257, it can be seen that for 62% of the respondents' preference for job has not changed. 12% of them are working as research scientists, 31% are working as consultants. For 69% of the doctors' present job is their first choice. 38% of the doctors belong to top levels of management in hospital. Very few responses were received when asked about break in their career.

35% of the respondents have refused their jobs, whereas 42% of the doctors have not refused. 40% of them say that they are expecting changes in next 5 to 10 years in their career. For 425 of the doctors' present job fulfils their expectations and aspirations, whereas 45% of the respondents are unhappy with their jobs.

TABLE - 4.243
CAREER CHOICE AND THE TYPE OF JOB

Reply	*Per cent*
Yes	64.0
No	26.0
No Reply	10.0
	100.0

Table 4.244 gives data about the choices about types of job. 10% didn't reply, 6% had desk type of job, 26% are having executive type of job and 57%.are in the last category.

TABLE - 4.244
CHOICES ABOUT THE TYPE OF JOB

Choice	*Per cent*
No Reply	10.0
Desk Type Job	. 06.0
Executive	26.0
Management	1.0
Any Other (like Hospital Administration, Social Welfare, etc.)	57.0
	100.0

TABLE - 4.245
CHANGE OF PREFERENCE

Change	*Per cent*
No Reply	9.0
Yes	29.0
No	62.0
	100.0

TABLE - 4.246
CURRENT PROFESSIONAL STATUS

Profession	*Per cent*
Practising Professionals	14.0
Consultancy	32.0
Executive/Manager	23.0
Industrialist/Entrepreneur	6.0
Academic Research/Teacher	12.0
Consultant (Employee)	1.0
Any Other	12.0
	100.0

Table 4.247 presents the data on nature of present job. 3% didn't reply, 48% are specialists, 42% are general physicians, 5% are consultants and 2% are in hospital administration.

TABLE - 4.247
NATURE OF PRESENT JOB OF THE RESPONSIBILITIES

Nature of Job	*Per cent*
No Reply	3.0
Specialist	48.0
General Physician	42.0
Consultant	5.0
Hospital Administration	2.0
	100.0

Table 4.248 gives the data on respondents' specific nature of job. 1% didn't reply, 17% are general physicians, 31% are consultants, 13% are in hospital administration and 38% are in any other category.

TABLE - 4.248
SPECIFIC NATURE OF WORK

Specification	*Per cent*
No Reply	1.0
General Physician	17.0
Consultant	31.0
Hospital Administration	13.0
Any Other Area of Specialization	38.0
	100.0

TABLE - 4.249
PRESENT JOB AS 1ST CHOICE

Reply	*Per cent*
No Reply	11.0
Yes	69.0
No	20.0
	100.0

TABLE - 4.250
CURRENT MANAGEMENT RESPONSIBILITIES

Level	*Per cent*
Top Level	38.0
Middle Level	36.0
Low Level	26.0
	100.0

Table 4.251 gives the data on break in the career of doctors. 74% didn't reply. 125 said yes and 14% said no when asked about this.

TABLE - 4.251
BREAK IN THE CAREER OF DOCTORS

Reply	*Per cent*
No Reply	74.0
Yes	12.0
No	14.0
	100.0

Table 4.252 gives data on the refusal of a job. 23% didn't reply, 35% said yes and 42% said no in their replies to this question.

TABLE - 4.252
REFUSAL OF A JOB BY THE RESPONDENTS

Reply	*Per cent*
No Reply	23.0
Yes	35.0
No	42.0
	100.0

TABLE - 4.253
CHANGES IN CAREER (NEXT FIVE TO TEN YEARS)

Reply	*Per cent*
No Reply	26.0
Yes	40.0
No	34.0
	100.0

Table 4.254 gives the data on respondents' present job fulfilments. 13% didn't reply. 42% said yes and 45% said no about this question.

TABLE - 4.254
PRESENT JOB FULFILS THE EXPECTATION AND ASPIRATIONS

Reply	*Per cent*
No Reply	13.0
Yes	42.0
No	45.0
	100.0

In Table 4.255 and 4.256 it can be seen that the attitude of the management has been based on merit and quality performed and is preferred as replied by 55% of the respondents, and for 20% is fair and just. 60% of the respondents say that any lapse on their part is being counselled. 23% of them give all the reasons when asked about their attitude towards the subordinate. The job is suited to their qualification for 26%, followed by 18% for whom doing the job is "in thing", 17% of the respondents are working under some influence, 5% are doing job under forced circumstances when asked about the factor influencing their decision for the present job.

TABLE - 4.255
ATTITUDE OF THE MANAGEMENT

Attitude	*Per cent*
No Reply	14.0
Fair and Just	20.0
Merit and Quality Performance given due Recognition	55.0
Different Treatment to Male/Female Counterpart	10.0
Not Fair	1.0
	100.0

Table 4.256 gives the data on respondents lapse while performing a job. 7% didn't reply, 30% say it is admonished, for 60% it is being counselled and 3% are ignored.

TABLE - 4.256
LAPSE ON THE PART OF THE RESPONDENTS

Lapse	*Per cent*
No Reply	7.0
Admonished	30.0
Counselled	60.0
Ignored	3.0
	100.0

Table 4.257 gives data regarding respondents' attitude towards subordinates. For 35% it is firm and official, 28% feel it is humane and concerned for their well-being, 14% feel it is participative and consultative and for 23% it is all the above four factors.

TABLE - 4.257
RESPONDENTS' ATTITUDE TOWARDS SUBORDINATES

Attitude	*Per cent*
Firm and Official	35.0
Humane and Concerned for their well-being	28.0
Authoritative and Demanding	0.0
Participative and Consultative	14.0
All Three Depending Upon the Situation	23.0
	100.0

Table 4.258 gives data on factors that influenced respondents' decision for the present job. For 26% it was qualification, for 5% it was circumstances, for 14% it was satisfaction, 17% say it was friend's/relation's/neighbour's influence, for 18% doing job is the "in thing", and 14% are working because of promotional avenues.

TABLE - 4.258
FACTORS THAT INFLUENCE THE DECISION FOR THE PRESENT JOB

Factor	*Per cent*
No Reply	6.0
Suited to my Qualification	26.0
Forced Circumstances	5.0
Satisfaction	14.0
Friend's/Neighbour's/Relation's/Influence	17.0
Doing a Job is the "In Thing"	18.0
Job has Promotional Avenues	14.0
	100.0

Socio-cultural Information

Tables 4.259 to 4.265 contain socio-cultural information about the respondents. 42% of the doctor respondents feel that woman as a mother has great responsibility towards rearing children. 48% of the respondents feel that only sometimes women have responsibility towards children. 65% of the respondents feel that society or organization does not provide adequate facilities for taking care of the children. 76% of the respondents feel that three months maternity leave is not sufficient for a working mother. The mother is working away for a number of hours from the house which has an effect on the development of the child was felt by 57% of the respondents.

TABLE - 4.259
DO WOMEN HAVE RESPONSIBILITY AS MOTHERS

Reply	*Per cent*
No Reply	3.0
Yes	42.0
No	7.0
Sometimes	48.0
	100.0

Table 4.260 gives the data on facilities for the upbringing of the children. 7% said yes, 28% said sometimes and 65% feel that society and organization don't provide any facilities for upbringing of children.

TABLE - 4.260
DO YOU HAVE FACILITIES FOR BRINGING UP CHILDREN

Reply	*Per cent*
Yes	7.0
Sometimes	28.0
No	65.0
	100.0

TABLE - 4.261
IS THREE MONTHS MATERNITY LEAVE ENOUGH

Reply	*Per cent*
Yes	17.0
No	76.0
No Reply	7.0
	100.0

TABLE - 4.262
IMPACT OF WORKING MOTHER'S ABSENCE FROM HOUSE

Any Impact	*Per cent*
Yes	57.0
No	43.0
	100.0

Tables 4.263 and 4.264 discuss the impact both negative and positive on the children. All the women think that there are both positive as well as negative impacts.

TABLE - 4.263
NEGATIVE IMPACT ON THE CHILDREN

Impact	*Per cent*
Health	57.0
Emotional Development	7.0
Mental Development	5.0
Shyness	3.0
All of the Above	28.0
	100.0

TABLE - 4.264

POSITIVE IMPACT ON THE CHILDREN

Impact	*Per cent*
Becomes Independent	4.0
Taking up Responsibility	13.0
More Sensible and Mature	10.0
More Intelligent	10.0
Extrovert	30.0
All the Above	33.0
	100.0

Table 4.265 presents the data on working persons and social obligation. 24% feel they do fulfil the obligation, 28% feel they don't and 48% feel that sometimes they fulfil the obligation.

TABLE - 4.265

WORKING PERSONS' SOCIAL OBLIGATION

Reply	*Per cent*
Yes	24.0
No	28.0
Sometimes	48.0
	100.0

In Tables 4.266 to 4.272, the data presented discuss the domestic information about their respondents. The married respondents did feel a change in division of labour in Indian Society. But 99% are unhappy with the existing division of labour in an Indian society. 100% of them feel that they should have a say in the decision making.

TABLE - 4.266

CHANGE IN DIVISION OF WORK OF HUSBAND/WIFE IN THE HOUSE

Reply	*Per cent*
Yes	57.0
Sometimes	26.0
No	17.0
	100.0

TABLE - 4.267
HAPPY WITH EXISTING DIVISION OF LABOUR IN INDIAN SOCIETY

Reply	*Per cent*
Yes	1.0
No	99.0
	100.0

Table 4.268 presents the data on respondents' view on the say of women in decision making in the house. 100% of them agreed for it.

TABLE - 4.268
SAY IN DECISION MAKING (OF THE HOUSE)

Reply	*Per cent*
Yes	100.0
	100.0

Table 4.269 discusses the decision-making areas. 1% focused on finance, 4% on the household decisions, 1% on the size of the family and 94% feel that it should be all of the above.

TABLE - 4.269
DECISION MAKING AREAS

Areas	*Per cent*
Finance	1.0
Household Decision	4.0
Size of the Family	1.0
All the above	94.0
	100.0

Tables 4.270 and 4.271 deal with respondents' views on Socio-cultural aspect. 85% of the total respondents were of the view that intercaste marriages are for better. They felt the reason for increase in divorce rate was due to adjustment problems as is the opinion of 53% of the women doctors.

TABLE - 4.270
INFLUENCE IN CAREER CHOICE

Relatives	*Per cent*
Parents	33.0
Brother/Sister	2.0
Your Own Choice	47.0
Teacher	1.0
Any Other Person	17.0
	100.0

Table 4.271 discusses the respondents' view on intercaste marriage, 85% feel it is for the better and 15% feel it is for the worst.

TABLE - 4.271
INTERCASTE MARRIAGE

Reply	*Per cent*
Better	85.0
Worst	15.0
	100.0

Table 4.272 discusses the respondents' view on rate of divorce. 53% feel it is due to adjustment problem and 28% feel it is due to changing position of women not being easily acceptable.

TABLE - 4.272
REASONS FOR INCREASE IN THE DIVORCE

Reasons	*Per cent*
Economic Independence	3.0
Self-awareness is Increasing	11.0
Age of Marriage is Increasing	5.0
Adjustment Problems	53.0
Changing Position of Women not Easily Acceptable	28.0
	100.0

Work Psychology

Tables 4.273 to 4.280 discuss work psychology of respondents. 62% of them feel that they are good job performers and 23% of them feel themselves as excellent job performers. 20% give emphasis on their happy family life. Exposure to new techniques and financial advancement were the primary sources of satisfaction in profession as was felt by 45% of the respondents. Parents' attitudes was responsible for low representation of women in medicine was felt by 40% of the respondents. 43% of the women feel that they can't cope up with family and job. 26% of them had no preference for men or women as far as subordinates and superiors were concerned. 40% of them did favour this field as a profession.

Table 4.273 discusses the reasons for their preference for work. 9% feel it is to earn money, for 20% it is better utilization of time, 31% feel it is meaning of life, 20% feel it gives better opportunities to spend time, for 20% it is a desire to do something in life.

TABLE - 4.273
REASONS FOR PREFERENCE FOR WORK

Reasons	*Per cent*
Earn Money	9.0
Better Utilization of Time	20.0
Meaning of Life	31.0
Better Opportunities to Spend Time	20.0
Desire to do Something in Life	20.0
	100.0

TABLE - 4.274
SELF-EVALUATION AT WORK

Evaluation	*Per cent*
Average Job Performer	15.0
Good Job Performer	62.0
Excellent Job Performer	23.0
	100.0

TABLE - 4.275
PRIMARY SOURCE OF SATISFACTION FOR WOMEN DOCTORS (IN PERSONAL LIFE)

Source	*Per cent*
Own Career Development	15.0
Happy Family Life	20.0
Growth and Development of Children	18.0
Any Other	20.0
	100.0

TABLE - 4.276
PRIMARY SOURCE OF SATISFACTION (IN PROFESSIONAL LIFE)

Source	*Per cent*
Exposure to New Techniques	20.0
Financial Advancement	25.0
Opportunity to Help the Country	15.0
Creative Activities	15.0
No Reply	25.0
	100.0

Table 4.277 discusses the reasons for low representation of women in the field, 40% feel it is due to parental discouragement, 20% feel it is because women are afraid of society's perception and 28% feel it is the tough competitions.

TABLE - 4.277
REASONS FOR LOW REPRESENTATION IN THE FIELD

Reason	*Per cent*
Most Parents Discourage their Daughters from taking up these Careers	40.0
Women are Afraid of Society's Perception	20.0
Society doesn't Accept this Profession	12.0
Tough Competitions	28.0
	100.0

Table 4.278 discusses the respondents' view on reasons for low representation in professional life. 13% feel the jobs are too demanding, 43% feel they cannot cope up with both the family and the job, for 12% it is difficulty in getting a suitable job and 32% say it is for different reasons.

TABLE - 4.278
REASONS FOR LOW REPRESENTATION IN PROFESSIONAL LIFE

Reason	*Per cent*
Jobs are Too Demanding	13.0
They cannot Cope up with Family and Job	43.0
Difficulty in getting a Suitable Job	12.0
Any Other	32.0
	100.0

Table 4.279 discusses doctors' preference about subordinates and superiors. 49% would prefer a woman. 25% feel that they would prefer a man and for 26% they didn't have any preference.

TABLE - 4.279
WOMEN DOCTORS' PREFERENCE

Preference	*Per cent*
Would Prefer a Woman	49.0
Would Prefer a Man	25.0
No Preference	26.0
	100.0

Table 4.280 discusses the advise by respondents to others. 40% feel it is "most certainly", 25% feel it is "yes", 31% feel it is "no" and 4% say it is "emphatically no".

TABLE - 4.280
ADVISE BY THE RESPONDENTS

Advise	*Per cent*
Most Certainly	40.0
Yes	25.0
No	31.0
Emphatically No	4.0
	100.0

Contrary to our belief that women educated in science and technology are emancipated, this study has further highlighted the role of social and socio-psychological factors in occupational choices and patterns of women with science and technology education. Social factors seem to play their roles starting from the early school days. However, teachers do not seem to play major role in the occupational choices though it is expected to be so. Most of the women of our study belong to fairly educated families except a few with social mobility to higher, technical-social group. Though the career choices are made at the secondary level by most of them, reasons for low representation of women seem to be originating from family itself. For quite a good number of these technical women, exposure to new knowledge is a source of satisfaction in professional life. The self-perception of their performance seems to be highly realistic. Most of them evaluated themselves as good performers in a four-point scale of poor to excellent performers. However, women also envisage their role as mothers is quite important and expect that proper arrangements are needed for day care of their children. Some of them feel that management attitude towards them is based on merit and quality. The facts emerging out of this study suggest that there is an urgent need for social change, i.e., change in the minds of people.

Women with career have to face a variety of problems. Keeping that in view it is very important to know the socio-cultural attitudes of the professionals. Almost 100% of the professionals agreed that woman as a mother has great responsibility towards rearing children and feels that neither society nor organization provides any facility for child care. They were of the view that three months maternity leave is not enough for them. 100% of the engineers, 98% of the architects and 57% of the doctors feel that long hours of absence of mother does have an impact on the children. But they agreed on both positive as well as negative impacts on the children. 33% of the total respondents feel that as a working person they are able to fulfil their social obligations. 38% of the respondents feel a change in the division of labour in Indian society. 100% of them agreed that woman should have a say in all areas in the decision making of the house. It is only engineers who have shown willingness to opt for different career in case of another opportunity.

Most women respondents have shown preference for inter-caste marriages, but feel adjustment problems and changing position of women not easily acceptable, are the two main reasons for increase in divorce rate in the country.

While discussing work psychology, the main reason for work is because it provides 'meaning to life' and consider themselves to be either good or excellent job performers. Amongst the various sources of satisfaction in their personal lives, happy family life and own career development are rated as primary sources. As far as professional life is concerned involvement in creative activity, financial advancement and exposure to creative activities are the source of satisfaction.

It is high time that various women's organizations, government and those interested in women's welfare should take adequate steps (1) to identify the occupations which are specially suitable for women (2) change the attitudes of men towards women, who play a major role in the development of children, (3) provide adequate guidance, right from the primary educational level, and give them necessary economic and other facilities of promoting higher education in different fields of science and technology, right up to doctoral level.

To conclude, changing social attitudes towards women, providing adequate guidance, help and encouragement and accepting them as equal partners in life and profession, will go a long way in promoting the case of women and their development.

FIVE

Factors Rrelated to Work Performance

Managerial approaches to work motivation have evolved along with the development of organizations at different times. Management philosophy initially developed with scientific management and human relations approach. The recent emphasis, however, is on the human potential and human resources approach. In Indian management style one finds a combination of scientific management principal and human relations approach, with little emphasis on human resources approach.

Until the latter part of the nineteenth century not much attention was paid to human factors in their contribution to industries. Workers were more or less treated like commodities, the idea that workers were like something that could be brought and only little attention was to be paid to them as individuals. This was the only way of managing an industry. Around the same time Taylor (1911) pioneered the "scientific management" movement. This movement aimed at systematizing managerial practices. He stressed on the need for standardization and control in operation of firms. Scientific management combines a study of physical capabilities of a worker (as is still done by industrial engineers in time and motion studies) coupled with an economic incentive approach. The central idea of the approach has been that, if material rewards are closely related to work efforts, the worker will respond with the maximum standard of job performance, he is physically capable of. Although Taylor originally started his study on the interaction between human characteristics and the characteristics of machine, the two elements which are major constituents of the industrial work process ended up by focusing on the physical characteristics of the human body in routine jobs. Taylor overlooked the social and psychological aspects of the job and the satisfaction a worker must get at work.

Human Relations Approach

In the early scientific management movement the employee was seen as primarily motivated by economic incentives. The managerial approach in industries took a turn and the most significant event which brought about a different view was the Hawthorne Studies from which emerged the idea that there is a relationship between productivity and attitudes of the employees. Mayo and his associates emphasized that a factory was a social system in itself, and group dynamics in the work situation had a vital role to play in industrial management. The industrial worker was then viewed as a human being with his attitudes, values, wants and desires influencing the effectiveness in the organization. They emphasized that amount of work carried out by a worker is not only determined by his physical capacity, as proposed by scientific management, but also by social factors. They also stressed on the importance of non-economic rewards in determining the motivation and happiness of workers. They also argued that the narrow specialization is by no means the most efficient form of division of labour. They viewed that workers do not react to management and its norms and individual rewards, so much as they do as group members. Thus the role of communication, participation and leadership are important factors in industrial management.

In spite of certain criticism on the methods of study used by Mayo and his associates, Hawthornes studies proved to be a landmark in ensuring human relations movement. Numerous studies to the aid of industrial world are being conducted by social scientists and surely this movement has crystallized into a body of knowledge in management of human resources. This approach has marked the origin of school though with emphasis on social concepts that have been useful in understanding the dynamics of human behaviour in organizations. These studies have uncovered the importance of social incentives in the workplace. They stress on the importance of human elements and social factors, contributing to productivity.

The human relation movement in industry emphasized on

creating a workforce with high morale and represented an attempt to breakdown formal boundaries that are part of the bureaucratic organization structure.

According to Knowles (1958) the human relations approach to the problems of industry asserts that some combinations of personalities, groups and organizations produce conflict, frustration and mental illness and that other combinations produce harmony satisfaction and mental health. The approach recognized that the human beings acquire definite attitudes. Thus, this is a tremendous contribution to industrial management science.

With the acceptance and importance of human relations movement, increasing emphasis has also been given to the worker as a whole man. No longer a worker is regarded solely as an economic tool. He is driven and controlled by diverse factors of environment and has expectations, desires and values. How he performs on his job depends on this total make up of personality to a great extent. This has given rise to human resource perspective of management.

Human Resources Approach

Organizational behaviour is a system consisting of the interacting elements of formal organization and human beings. Individual interacts with this formal organization to satisfy his needs that impinge on his total personality. Consequently the behavioural outcomes in the organization reflects as much the dynamics of the organization as the modification of individual's behaviour in terms of need satisfaction.

A given work situation has three important aspects, i.e., structure of its own, its own process of communication and decision making and application of certain technique or knowledge in work. In the process of interaction with the work situation, the individual tries to satisfy his needs involving his own personality. Consequently, it is a question of the change the individual undergoes to modify has behaviour in the organization. Thus, the total output of his behaviour is a function of the inputs that the formal organization provides him with and the pattern of psychological processes that work within him. With the growth of the human relations movement, increasing emphasis has been given to the worker as a whole man. No longer is he viewed solely as an economic tool, but as a human being, who is driven and controlled by diverse elements of society and has fears, frustrations, desires, values, and expectations which affect his total personality. How he performs on his job, i.e., his efficiency and productivity, are dependent as much, if not more, on the external aspects surrounding his workplace, as on the tools and materials he uses. Therefore, it must be recognized that man as a worker is unique compared to other resources of the organization. He must be motivated not only to do his job but to strive constantly to improve his performance. This then, remains the cardinal objective of the human relations functions to discover the newer and better ways of understanding man and his work behaviour so as to help people to realize their maximum potential.

The assumption of human relations approach has been challenged by a number of researchers, who have highlighted the human resources approach. This is not an oversimplified approach like human relations approach. This views that human beings are motivated by a complex set of interrelated factors. These factors take into account the enormous talent and potential an individual brings to his workplace with him. It is a question of giving him opportunities to utilize his talent, creativity and potentials by giving him a meaningful work assignment and by adding greater responsibility, autonomy, variety, etc.

Motivation and job performance has received considerable attention in Indian industries in recent years among practising managers, industrial/organizational psychologists and policy makers. This has become a focal point of interest, in view of our concern for productivity and effective organizations. For such a concern perhaps, it becomes important for any organization to attract good employees who could perform the task in dependable manner and also use their creativity, innovation in their job performance. On the other hand, the organization should offer them a working culture, a climate that enhances their growth and fulfils their expectations. Perhaps giving financial incentives is just one aspect of the whole process. This reason gives the feeling that motivational problems are the central theme in the psychology of job performance leading to effective organizations.

Motivation concept is a highly complex phenomenon that affects and is affected by a large number of factors in the person-organization system. The concept has been defined by many researchers as an inner state that energizes, moves or activates the behaviour of an individual. This has also been defined as a process of governing choices among many forms of activities. In this study, employee's motivation to work has been analysed. An attempt has been made to study the job performance of industrial worker, within the framework of a proposed cognitive theory of work motivation. Such a framework would help us in organizing our thoughts concerning human performance. The conceptional model proposed makes three assumptions. Firstly, employee motivation for job performance is a complex phenomenon, which cannot be properly understood without a multivariate approach. Secondly, employee perception of the job situation and his expectancies and way of viewing the world is important. Every worker views his work situation through his subjective world. Thirdly, motivationally important factors may be viewed within a system analysis perspective.

Within the multivariate research framework, employees personality and backward variables have been studied as two groups of factors, and his perception of the organizational climate variables has been studied as the third group of factors. Cognitive approach to work, motivation and the system's approach taken in the study, are discussed in the next few pages.

The human relations researcher views human behaviour, whether at the individual or at the social level, as developing within an interacting framework in which each part influences every other part in a dynamic way. Bakke (1959) defines an organization as a continuing system which is able to differentiate and integrate human activities which utilize, transform and weld together a set of human material and other resources into a problem solving whole. The function of the organization is to satisfy particular human needs in interaction with other subsystems of human activities in particular environment.

The basic concept was well described by Henderson (1936) who pointed out that the interdependence of the variables in a system is one of the widest inductions (inferences) from experience that we possess, or we may alternatively regard it as a definition of a system. Huse and Bowditch (1973) define the system as a series of interrelated and interdependent parts, such that the interaction on any of the subsystems affect the whole. Infact, systems approach views interactions and interdependence among subsystems are as important as the individual components. It affects the performance of the entire system.

Boulding (1956) pointed out different levels of system ranging from static structure to dynamic structure and human systems. He believes that human systems and social systems are the most complicated ones and we have yet to discover the rudiments of theoretical models for them.

An organization is an open behaviour system with a number of interdependent subsystems. Each subsystem can be considered as a system in its own right as well as a total system. Each worker is one of the important subsystem within the organization and affects the whole unit in different degrees through his performance. It is found that the worker, similar to a social system is a complex one in himself consisting of multitude of subsystems acting on inputs, received from outside the world, seeks balance between his desire and need for growth and self-fulfilment.

One may look at the human system from psychological perspective. The important variables are worker's attitude, motivation, values and norms of behaviour and these will interact with each other. Most of the social systems have multiplicity of subsystems for study and enlarge our analysis from micro to macro level.

In industrial context some of the motivating factors for good job performance reported, are supervisory style, wages, fringe benefits, working conditions, decision-making opportunities, promotional opportunities, etc. There seems to be multiplicity of different sources of satisfaction and dissatisfaction intrinsic to job performance, which are functions of both characteristics of the person performing it, i.e., his personality (Vroom, 1964).

Industrial organizations, though commonly characterized by their physical structure, are psycho-social systems. An industrial organization functions successfully only when the people filling each structural position, perform their roles in a dependable manner. Behaviour of a skilled worker within an organization setting represents an interaction between the behavioural demands of the task situation and the behavioural requirements that the individual has for himself. Thus, given a job, there are a variety of questions that one can ask about his accomplishment and effectiveness at the job. Survey of the studies reported reveal that job performance is a result of many interrelated and complex set of variables. It is thus necessary to explore total situation in assessing this job linked behaviour as far as possible as already discussed in the conceptual framework for the study and depicted in the model.

Ability and Motivation as Joint Determinants of Performance

The assumption of job performance as a result of ability multiplied by motivation has led to efforts to measure abilities and motivation as determinants of job performance. The term "ability" usually denotes a potential for performing some task. A person's ability to perform a task refers to the degree to which he possesses all the psychological attributes necessary for a high level of performance excluding those of motivational nature. Vroom (1960) reported high positive correlation between, and zero or slightly negative correlation for those low in it.

Joint effects of intelligence and achievement motivation on problem solving success of airmen have found a significant interaction between these variables. Among those subjects who were high in motivation, performance was positively related to their intelligence. A study of airforce trainees suggested that performance was significantly higher under high motivation conditions. However, the difference in performance between the two motivation conditions was significantly greater for subjects high in ability (as measured by previous performance on the task) (French, 1975, Flaishman, 1958).

Vitles (1953) used the terms like "capacity to work" and "will to work" and had proposed that both determine the level of performance. Muthayya (1962) studied intelligence of high and low achievers in the scholastic field in a group of thirty boys and found a lack of relationship between achievement and intelligence. Vroom (1964) has suggested that if an interaction between ability and motivation were to be corroborated in further research, it would have considerable implications for managerial practice.

In the present study, occupational skills and education have been kept constant by selecting the skilled workers with specialized industrial training diploma (ITI). Intelligence as a variable has also been included in the study.

Relationship of Motivation to Personality

The way a given motive is manifested in behaviour is a function of the particular personality constellation in which it is embedded. Expressions of the attitudes are influenced by many variables including motivation and personality. The concept of 'cognitive control' has been used to refer to a manner or style of performance which reflects in a number of situations. Perhaps the effects of any motive are filtered through the constraint provided by personality controls. This is to say that controls in a subject's personality will moderate the way he responds to need and the way motive is reflected in behaviour. Such findings suggest that while tracing out motivational effects in behaviour of people the personality and other variables must be taken into consideration. According to Cofer and Appley (1964), the expression of motivation in adult human beings is modulated in all probability by personality mechanism, so that the direct evidence of motivational factors is seldom seen.

No two persons have exactly the same mixture or strength of these needs and personality. There are some people who are driven mainly by money, others are primarily concerned with security, and so on. While individual differences including gender must be recognized, it does not mean that predictions about the motive which seems to be currently more prominent among employees cannot be made. They further point out that individuals act on the basis of their perceptions and expectation not on reality. By bringing reality and their perception closer, a manager can increase the effectiveness of the employees.

Motivation, embedded in worker's personality, background characteristics and attitudes may affect the employee's job performance. Present investigation throws light mainly on some background, psychological and attitudinal variables as related to job performance. Apart from these random variables, a fixed variable, i.e., the ownership of the company (private or public sector) has also been included in the study.

Relationship between an individual's demographic characteristics and job performance may suggest that people with similar backgrounds have similar behaviour structure. Herman and Hulin (1972) demonstrated that, within the same organization, demographic background accounted for a significant and substantial portion of the variance in response to the work environment. Background factors included in this study are age, experience, sex, matérial status, tenure in the present organization, socio-economic status and income.

Herzberg et. al. (1959) suggests that the younger men more frequently perceived the intrinsic characteristics of the work itself as a reason for lack of motivation than older ones in their sample. In general, older group reported high morale. Sinha and Agrawal (1971) concluded that older workers had better job motivation than younger ones. Herman Dunham and Hulin (1975) reported that older employees who were the primary wage earners in their families appeared to have high level of job involvement. This study identified young male employees as being less satisfied with their supervisor and experiencing low level of job involvement and motivation. Taylor (1975) examined the influence of age on performance in decision making on a sample of industrial managers. Age was found to influence the performance in decision making.

House (1974) found that, when females were in competitive situation, they showed lower expectancies for their performances than did males. Deaus and Emswiller (1974) reported that good performance by females are more likely to be attributed to luck. Similar results are reported by Feldman, Summers and Kiehers (1974) in study of attribution of occupational success. Matteson and McMohan (1974) reported significant differences between the two sexes as regards their job attitudes. Frienze (1975) also found that there are differences in casual attribution for success and failure in males and females.

Men generally attribute their success to stable factors such as ability, and failure to luck. The pattern is reverse in case of women.

This relationship, however, is moderated by individual differences in achievement motivation. These findings may have implications for job performance as well.

With the dual role of career making and home making for women, it is quite likely that need patterns and motivation forces influencing job performance may not follow same pattern for males and females. In recent years, in India, with possible entry of women on industrial scene, this concept becomes more interesting. This field has not been probed deeply in the Indian context.

Generally, managers feel that pay is the most important aspect of job motivation. Herzberg's theory (Herzberg et al., 1959) stresses its role as hygiene factor, although Lawler (1973) indicates that it can serve as a motivator of job performance.

Earlier, Whyte (1955) stressed that there is no doubt that money has an important effect on behaviour of production workers, but this effect is neither as simple nor as strong as management has often assumed.

Experience is cumulative learning, in the sense that each new situation is inevitably dealt with in terms of previous experience. Past experience usually assists in the new working situation of the similar type improving the speed and accuracy of dealing with the job resulting in better accomplishment of job. But the relationship does not seem to be just and simple. Kohn and Schooler (1973) studied the relationship between man's occupational experience and his psychological functioning and suggested that these result from a continuing interplay between job and man, in which the effects of job on man are far from trivial.

Study of socio-economic status has become important with shift of workers from rural to urban industrialized cities in India, it is only after India's independence that industrial townships have started coming up, transforming nearby villages into towns. Generally, farm workers have changed their occupation and have joined the industrial force. Such a transformation in society made impact on the socio-economic status of the industrial workers. This fact is likely to make some reflection on the job performance of the workers.

Tenure in the corporation according to Herman, Dunham and Hulin (1975) is descriptive of the direct employee-organization interface. Thus, this background variable may influence employee motivation in terms of job performance.

Herman, Dunham and Hulin (1975) also found that persons with similar demographic characteristics like age, sex, and marital status reported similar degree of satisfaction and job involvement and experienced similar levels of motivation. The unique relationship between demographic characteristics and psychological responses suggests that employees perceive work experience through the lens of their own value system.

Attitudes towards Organization and Organizational Climate

Attitudes are the tendencies to respond positively or negatively towards any person, object or situation. According to Guilford (1971), motivations are manifested in attitudes. This being so, the knowledge of attitudes may help in the prediction of behaviour in industry. Attitudes are related to values, internal needs, level of aspirations, expectations and motivations of the individual worker.

According to Herzberg et. al. (1959), the problem of people's relationship with their work continues to be a basic one and attitudes towards the job exert an extremely important influence on the way the job was done.

Even (1976) has emphasized the importance of attitudes as organizational climate perception. According to him, organizational climate is a multinational perception by members as well as non-members of the essential attributes or character of an organizational system.

He further points out that organizational members tend to perceive the climate differently and this perception whether real or unreal has behaviour consequences for the organization.

Lawler (1968) examined the relationship expectancy attitude and job performance. The model relates motivation, social needs, and obtains his basic sense of identity through relationship with others. He further points out that man is more responsive to the social forces of the peer group than incentives, and he is responsive to the management only to the extent he feels that his social needs of belongingness and acceptance are met. Maslow (1943) has also stressed the importance of need for belongingness in industrial motivation.

Some Personality Correlates of Job Performance

Behaviour is governed not by objective facts, but by the facts as perceived by individual. According to Stagner (1956) each person sees the world in a manner slightly more different than others. These differences are results of unique individual personality and psychological make up. A job which is satisfying and motivating to one person may often be boring to others. Individual differences in need strengths may be related to some personality characteristics of the workers result in different motivation.

Saunders and Stanton (1976) attempted to find unique patterns of personality traits which are associated with various performance styles. Using canonical correlation analysis three separate performance styles were extracted with sets of personality traits. The author concluded that concern should be placed on their psychological set since it plays an important role in their process of global attainment.

In this investigation, locus of control, values and occupational aspirations have been studied as variables related to job performance and as intervening variables between perception of organizational climate and job performance.

Locus of control (Rotter, 1966) is a personality dimension related to an individual's attempt to master the environment. In the framework of Rotter's (1966) social learning theory, internal-external locus of control refers to the degree to which an individual perceives success and failure as being contingent upon personal initiative. To one end of the internal-external continuum are the highly internals, i.e., those who perceive effort to be largely instrumental in attaining success. At the other end of the spectrum are the highly, externals those who attach no values to initiative and view the success as completely uncorrelated to ability and efforts. Internals thus believe that they control the fate, whereas externals feel that they are controlled by it.

Although the literature on internal-external control has given little attention to this variable it relates to job performance its construction is particularly well suited for predicting employment success and job performance. Research studies reported by Joe (1971), Lefcourt (1966, 1972) and Rotter (1966, 1972) contain strong evidence that an internal expectancy reflects a propensity to influence one's environment. Internals believe that success results from hard work. Lefcourt (1972) considers this factor as offering considerable support for a theoretically provable relationship between effectiveness and increased perceptions of personal controls. In spite of voluminous literature on locus of control, not many research efforts have been made to explore the role of this variable in the dynamics of work experience. Broedlilg (1975) studied relationship between job performance and locus of control. His hypothesis that internal locus of control will be related to the work motivation and job performance were confirmed at .05 significance level.

Andirsoni and Nestel (1976) examined the influence of internal-external control on a number of facets of work experience. The study concluded that data provided considerable support for the hypothesis that success at work enhances the expectancy of internal controls. Noditch and Demaio (1975) studied relationship between locus of control and effective performance in schools. Results indicated that, among males, locus of control was significantly related to competent performance only among those subjects who placed a high value on outcome in each area. Among females the pattern was exactly the reverse.

Level of Occupational Aspirations

How the individual sets his goal and reacts to his own performance is an important factor determining prediction of his job success, the profess of goal setting, or the level of aspiration was first emphasized by Lewin (1935). A quite widely accepted generalization from experiments on level of aspiration is that successful performance leads to an increased level of aspiration and unsuccessful one leads to reduced level (Lewin et. al., 1944).

There are probably differences among situations in the ways in which various factors influence subjective probabilities on the one hand and incentive values on the other. Vroom (1964) stated that there have been no such investigation in industrial situations.

Values

Values play a central role in our lives; a good deal of our behaviours are based upon values we hold. Every decision we make contains both factual and value elements. Workers in industry also behave in accordance with how they perceive the job situation. According to Krech, Churchfield and Balleachery (1962), people construct a "cognitive image or map" of their world. Behaviour is the result of such perceptions.

Bertalanffy (1964) pointed out that values are things or acts which are chosen by and are desirable to an individual within a certain frame of reference. He further points out that we obviously will have to include both objects and acts while studying value patterns. Material things like dollars or a Picasso painting and the charitable acts also stress different values. These performances affect the behaviour of an individual.

Tolman (1951) stressed on belief-value matrix, which may be culturally shared or unique to an individual. It consists of beliefs that doing things or getting to objects, situations, or goals, will experience and may function as an instrumentality in the service of needs.

Littman (1958) refers to values as a motivational term, because it designates something that is active rather than passive. Measured values and preferences have practical utility in predicting other behaviour (Coffer and Appley, 1964).

Value, according to Vroom (1964) refers to preference like valence; but it is broader in nature and refers to the strength of desires of aversions for large classes of outcomes. In this study Allport-Vernon-Lindzey (1951) scale of values has been used. This scale, based on Spranger's classification of values, provides data on six value dimensions; theoretical economics, social, religious, aesthetic and political. Vernon and Allport (1931) compared the scores on Allport-Vernon value scale of persons working in different fields and found that, in general, these groups were congruent with the nature of their chosen professions. Though the construct suggested by Allport-Vernon-Lindzey has been used as a motivational force in many fields it has not been studied generally with reference to employee's job performance in industries.

According to Sikula (1971), values and value systems are merely priority patterns of values along continuum of importance. More insightful analysis of motivated behaviour can be made through the use of value concept. He further points out that study of value is a new and promising approach to explain motivated behaviour. Value analysis can be used to understand not only individual behaviour but group and organizational behaviour as well.

Job Satisfaction and Job Performance

The extent to which a worker strives to perform effectively in a job, is not solely a function of his personality or of the nature of his work role but is a complex resultant of both types of variables. The argument that worker's satisfaction and his motivation to perform effectively should be viewed as a joint function of situational and personality variables, by no means implies that their determinants are identical (Vroom, 1964). Generally, very low correlation between job performance and job satisfaction reported in researches also throws light on this issue. Katz, Maccoby, Gurin and Floor (1951) reported no relationship between job performance and job satisfaction. Brayfield and Crockett (1955) concluded that there was little evidence of any simple or appreciable relationship between employee's attitude and job performance. Landy (1969), Pritchard (1969), Comisarow (1970) and Huber (1970) in their various studies have analysed variables like motivations, superior-subordinate relationship and challenge in relation to job satisfaction and job performance. They observed that such variables did not show similar pattern of relationship to job satisfaction and job performance.

Korman (1968) found that subject's self-esteem moderated the relationship between task success (performance) and task likes (satisfaction). Vecchio (1980) has indicated that moderator hypothesis is valid for worker anomie, education and type of residence.

Hulin (1971) and Hackman and Lawer (1971) have demonstrated that job satisfaction and other favourable outcomes are primarily characteristics of those who desire satisfaction of higher order needs. This motivational moderator appears to provide for more precise prediction than moderators of sociological nature.

The study of Indian workers' relationship among background variables, personality variables, job satisfaction and organizational perception variables have been analysed in relation to their job performance.

An analysis of commitment process is also presented. The relationship between background variables and job performance has been presented in Table 5.1.

TABLE - 5.1
RELATIONSHIP BETWEEN BACKGROUND VARIABLES AND JOB PERFORMANCE OF INDUSTRIAL WORKERS

Variable	*r for male workers (N=353)*	*r for female workers (N=44)*
Age	-.031	-.180
Marital Status	-.061	.078
Experience	-.026	-.036
Present Tenure	.037	-.056
SEES	.137	.061
Income	.106	.123

The pattern of correlations indicate that none of the correlations are statistically significant for female employees, whereas in case of males, income and socio-economic status are significant at 5% level of significance. Table 5.2 presents the attitude towards work and job performance.

TABLE - 5.2
RELATIONSHIP BETWEEN ORGANIZATION CLIMATE PERCEPTION AND JOB PERFORMANCE

Attitudes	*Males (N=353)*	*Females (n=44)*
Job Satisfaction	.089	-.298*
Perception of Self-development Opportunities	-.100	-.145
Feeling of Belongingness	-.093	.118
Attitude towards Working Conditions	.102	-.017
Attitude towards Supervision	-.010	-.200
Attitude towards Financial Benefits	-.037	.094
Attitude towards Employment Security	.071	-.057
Attitude towards Interaction and Consideration Opportunities	.172**	.299*
Attitude towards Self-esteem and Consideration	.172**	-.260

* $P < .05$
** $P < .01$

It is observed from the Table 5.3 that there is a negative relationship between job performance and job satisfaction in case of female workers. Male workers show a positive relationship (r=.102) with attitude towards working conditions. Perception of interaction opportunities has positive correlation with job performance amongst both groups.

Attitude towards self-esteem and consideration shows significant positive relation in case of males, but negative trend towards closeness of supervision, though the value of correlation is not very high. Attitude towards financial benefits does not show any significant relationship with the level of job performance in both cases.

TABLE - 5.3

CORRELATIONS BETWEEN PERSONALITY VARIABLES AND JOB PERFORMANCE OF MALE AND FEMALE WORKERS

Variable	*Males (N=353)*	*Females (N=44)*
Locus of Control	.223*	-.048
Level of Occupational Aspiration	.468**	.435**
Religious Value	-.150**	.074
Aesthetic Value	.057	-.0245
Political Value	-.005	-.113
Theoretical Value	.135*	.385*
Economic Value	.031	-.183
Social Value	.029	.310

* P < .05

** P < .01

Pattern of correlation suggests that there is high positive relationship between internal locus of control and the level of job performance in case of male employees (r= .203), whereas females do not show any significant relationship between these two variables.

The findings consist of some reported researches. Nowicki (1973) reported that externality was associated with achievement for females (r= .39, N=.26) while internality was related to achievement for males (r= -.50, N = 22). Noditch and Demaio (1975) in study of school performance and locus of control, also indicated similar results.

Level of occupational aspirations shows high positive correlation with the level of job performance. In case of male workers, relationship seems to be slightly higher (r = .468) than female workers (r = .435). Religious value has a significant negative correlation with the job performance (r = .140) in case of male workers, but not in case of females. Theoretical value shows a high correlation with the level of job performance in case of women workers (r = .385). Male workers also show a positive relationship of this variable with job performance (r = .138). Other values do not seem to have obvious relationship with the level of job performance.

Productivity and Job Satisfaction

Correlation coefficients between job satisfaction and job performance range between .041 to .298 as revealed from the Table 5.3.

TABLE - 5.3
THE RELATIONSHIP BETWEEN JOB SATISFACTION AND JOB PERFORMANCE FOR VARIOUS SAMPLES

Male Sample (N = 353)	-.089
Female Sample (N = 44)	-.298*
Public Sector (N = 139)	.042
Private Sector (N = 258)	-.190**

* P < .05
** P < .01

Hackman and Lawler (1971) report a positive correlation among job motivation, satisfaction and performance only for employees reporting satisfaction of higher order needs, i.e., need for accomplishment, growth, challenge and participation.

Vroom (1964) analysed data from 20 studies exploring relationship between job performance and job satisfaction and pointed out that there was a range in value of correlations and coefficients. The analysis reveals that work psychology of women employees is different than that of men. Therefore there is need to redesign work systems keeping in view there gender differences. This strategic factor if managed effectively can make the organizations effective.

The Concept of Commitment

"Commitment highlights one of the ways in which individuals infuse roles and social structures with self-motivated behaviour" (Burke and Reitzes, 1991). Foote (1951) introduced the concept of commitment and argued that role playing and one's full commitment to one's identity are essential for an active self. Commitment creates a link between the individual and society. Theoretical concepts of commitment including work by Becker (1960), Stryker (1968, 1982) and Kanter (1968, 1972) focuses on commitment as a tie between an individual and either a line of activity, or a particular role partner of an organization. Commitment can be of different types, namely, work commitment, organizational commitment, job commitment, interpersonal commitment, family commitment and so on.

An approach based on identity theory or affect control theory suggests that commitment connects an individual to an identity. Beckor further focused attention on the social psychological processes involved in commitment. He points out that active individuals not only internalize role expectations but work out the behavioural implications of roles and role boundaries.

Safilios-Rothschild (1970) defines commitment as the investment of time, interest, energy and emotions in a particular area related to other areas of life. At times commitment is used interchangeably with words like job satisfaction, work involvement, motivation and even morale. Greenberger and Goldberg, 1989; Greenberger and O'neil (1990, 1993) assessed role commitment on three major dimensions, that is, centrality of the role to the self; salience of the particular role vis-a-vis other activities and desire to perform well in that role. Commitment can be of different types, namely, work.

Harmon (1970) reported that highly committed women were found to differ from others only in the years of education and years of work experience they had. It was found that these women did not differ in satisfaction with home making and hours spent in voluntary activities. They had higher educational level (though not necessarily brighter than less committed women). Reasons for commitment were found to be motivational not circumstantial, Bailyn (1978) emphasizes that working couples face the complications of defining the relationship between work and family and has described the patterns of accommodation to resolve this issue in a way that is congruent with the other's commitment.

Welsch and Lavan (1981) studied Interrelationship among organizational commitment and job characteristics, job satisfaction, professional behaviour and organizational climate. They observed that organizational commitment is an important behaviour dimension which can be utilized to evaluate employees' strength of attachment. Results indicated that role conflict and role ambiguity are detrimental to commitment while a participative climate, power, team, work, reading professional journals, satisfaction with work and performance opportunities, age, tenure and length of professional employment are positively related to organizational commitment.

A study of 473 members of the Canadian forces (232 men and 241 women) found considerable difference between men and women in levels of burnout organizational commitment and psychosomatic symptoms. Work environments into which women had been recently introduced were considered by both men and women to be impoverished in terms of support systems women found these environments to provide fewer coping resources. The results supported a prediction that supportive collegial relationship were of greater salience to women than to men and that women were more concerned with issues of powerlessness when confronting organizational problems.

It is felt that in India, researches on dual role of women are not comprehensive, as is also stressed by Jaiprakash (1985). Empirical investigations on commitment are scarce and scattered. The field of women, work and work commitment is still largely unexplored and provides a rich ground for researches. Future research on commitment of mothers must include both work and family related factors. Related researches on commitment have not been able to include all the dimensions involved. They must include aspects such as health role strain, type of work, time scheduling of work whether fixed or flexible, type of family: joint or nuclear, family environment, quality of work life, time taken to reach to the workplace, perception of job satisfaction, child care facilities, support services, researches, etc. These would be very helpful for implementers at the governmental level for the optimum growth of human resources.

This section has focused on the factors related to work performance and gender. It may be observed that work designs for women need greater attention of policy makers enhancing contributions of women for national development. Further this is an agenda for the strategic Human Resource Management and needs to be paid due attention.

helpful for implementing the governmental laws for the optimum growth of human resources.

This section has focused on the factors related to work performance and gender. It may be inferred that such measures for women need greater attention of policy makers [illegible] contribution of women for national development. Human [illegible] is an agenda for the strategic Human Resource Management and needs to be paid due attention.

SIX

Work Designs

There are several approaches to work design starting from the days of early industrialization. The scientific management approach emphasized on the national economic assumption about human nature and work design. Later, approaches like human engineering, job rotation, job enlargement, job enrichment and goal setting were emphasized. After the humanistic school of thought, self-actualizing assumptions and quality of work life approaches were proposed. These approaches stress on democracy at the place of work, creativity and humanization of work as a whole. This chapter presents the role of quality of work life and work life of women workers.

The world of work in a modern industrial setting is different. Employee's work lives today are affected by complex interdependence of factors characterized by productive processes. For efficiency's sake the tasks are usually broken down into smaller operations repeated over and over throughout the workday. Modern industry is characterized by a situation in which morale of the employee's is threatened by impersonal character of the work itself. Feeling of injustice and unfair treatment at the place of work has also received attention of researchers.

Awareness of such human issues and the interest in improving the quality of worklife (QWL) have led to the QWL programmes. QWL research is concerned with how the relationship between individuals and features of their physical, social and economic work environment affects those on and off attitudes and behaviours. An essential aspect of QWL programme is the opportunity for individuals or task groups at any level to influence their working environment to have some say over what goes on in connection with their work. Some subsidiary elements involved in programmes designed to enhance QWL are—achieving sustained commitment from management to an open style of operation which includes information sharing, consultation and feeling of equity. Quality of work life as a job design include establishment of an environment that encourages continuous learning and training, affording opportunities for continuous growth and training of supervisors for greater efficiency, etc.

For increasing quality of working life and for job enrichment a number of action researches have been conducted in India. De (1976) has emphasized on the participative work design and redesigning of work. De and Srivastava are the first to contribute in the form of reports which appear in this area in India. Srivastava in his paper "Continuous and Organization of Work" has traced the current statutes and future implication for increasing quality of working life and job enrichment as well through redesigning of work. In his paper the author has highlighted the importance of workplace, of institutions of work and importance of work in life. Highlighting the social and economic relations, he has given two cases of work redesign. One action research was conducted by National Labour Institute in collaboration with client organizations. The project was undertaken for detailed analyses of at least two work design projects in terms of the felt need for change, the dynamics change process and the outcomes. These researchers have discussed in length about these projects. The first case refers to the work redesign, project undertaken in a fabrication shop of a heavy industry plant. There the redesigning of the work system was introduced and the results were very encouraging. The productivity increased, absenteeism during summer season also minimized.

In his paper "Quality of Working Life and Work Environment" De, has talked about relationship among "Work", "Life" and "Environment" and has proposed the process of increasing QWL as:

(a) Variation and meaningful tasks for one and all sweeper upwards,
(b) by creating opportunities for learning and continuous and permanent education,

(c) by providing increased autonomy,
(d) by augmenting social support in collaborative work groups instead of establishment of fierce competition, as has been the contribution of some cultures,
(e) bringing about meaningful relations between job and the social environment, and
(f) provision for desirable career patterns for one and all and not only for managers.

Quality of life, however, is dependent on the QWL. Life without work has no meaning and work which is meaningless is a low QWL and that consequently brings about a low ability of life. QWL is an indicator of how free the society is from exploitation, injustice, oppression and restriction on the continuing growth of man, leading to his development to the fullest structure.

Taking into consideration the role of national economy, market economy, values of elitism and so many other factors, number of strategies are proposed to increase the quality of life. An experiment in attitude change reveals that during the study in which managers, supervisors and workers were also involved, had fragmented work system, with each one concerned with his own trade. In the first place, none of the workers were emotionally or rationally committed. Secondly, there was idle time invariably because when a particular worker was working at a spot, another worker with a different trade could not take up his job. Thirdly, having worked on the same trade over a number of years, the fragmented job itself did not provide any challenge to the workers themselves.

A Study of Women Industrial Workers

This section is addressed to the understanding of the principles underlying the humanization of work and their relationship with job performance of industrial workers. The principles of security, equity, individuation and democracy, which altogether underline the humanization of work have been studied along with the job performance of 81 women workers of an industry manufacturing meters of different types. In case of equity and individuation there is a negative relationship with job performance; whereas the democracy at the place of work has positive relationship with job performance. The study thus highlights the quality of working life and organization design as important dimensions of organization functioning.

In the literature of industrial psychology, there is a growing evidence to show that job designs and organizational designs are key factors in determining an employee's work behaviour. Therefore an important goal of an organization and society is to design and develop organizations and jobs in such a way that they enhance and stimulate the creative abilities of workers. This is likely to give them the opportunities of self-development, self-actualization and positive attitudes towards work and life. This is referred to as humanization of work. However as a society we seem to be far from achieving the goal. The reasons are rooted in the overall social attitudes of managers. For example, profit is considered as the only goal of an industry and worker's well-being are considered as waste of money. The employee's are treated like machines. Managers unfortunately overlook the intangible gains that the positive quality of life may have. Often unions also limit their attempts to humanize only security or equity factors. However designing humanized work systems remains a challenge in most of the organizations. In recent years workers are becoming aware of their rights and this may promote humanization of work to some extent. It is also hoped that the professionally trained new managers will pay attention to full human development.

Therefore, there is always a question of worker's productivity linked with humanization of work. This is perhaps more important for the women force who with the changing work values no longer consider money or to earn as the main purpose of their career, for many of them, work is in quest of self-development and self-actualization. A modest attempt has been made to study the perception of humanization of work by women industrial workers and their job performance. It is therefore hypothesized that there is a positive relationship between the perception of humanization of work and job performance.

Herzberg's job enrichment theory states that the factors responsible for enrichment of job are responsibility autonomy, variety, nature of work, etc. Maslow (1943) in his theory of need hierarchy has stated that higher order needs are the need for self-esteem and self-actualization which are the growth needs.

Therefore, these needs must be reasonably satisfied for self-actualization. Herrick and Maccoby (1975) have observed that humanizing work through optimization of workers' well-being is the priority goal of organizations. He has suggested the four principles of humanization of work as security, equity, individuation and workplace democracy.

Principle of Security

According to this principle the need of worker's to be free from any anxiety or fear is an important determinant of humanization of work. This ear/anxiety could be at the place of work in the form of income, job security, safety and dangerous physical conditions, physical security, etc.

The Principle of Equity

This principle refers to the concept of paying worker which will commensurate with his skill abilities and knowledge in comparison with other organizations. Therefore the principle implies that employees should be compensated commensurately with their contribution to the value of a service and concern for fairness at work.

The Principle of Individuation

Since an employee spends larger part of his working life at the place of work, his work must give him opportunities to stimulate the development of unique abilities, craftsmanship and continued learning. This concern will encourage human development and the organization as a whole. Recent studies have revealed that desire for autonomy, responsibility, interesting jobs are important factors in work motivation. Fromm (1973) has emphasized that both psychological and physiological studies show a direct relationship between boredom and destructiveness in people.

The Principle of Democracy

In recent years managers have started realizing the importance of involving workers in decision making or what is called Participative Management. This principle ranges from information sharing to direct control of the enterprise by workers. Thus a structure is created to institutionalize the responsibility and authority of workers.

This system of the four principles optimizes the worker's well-being, hope and mental health in general, leading to better quality of working life. This in turn also helps in development of a healthy society.

The Study

The study has been conducted with survey research design in a meter manufacturing industry of Faridabad (Haryana). The study includes all the female employees of this factory present at the time of study (N=175). The age range is between 20 to 49 years. They are all married, not highly educated working as unskilled and skilled workers, clerks, etc. There was no woman manager in the organization. Data were collected on the following variables:

(a) Data on the perception of equity, security, individuation and participation were collected by a questionnaire prepared by the authors. The test-retest reliability of this questionnaire is 86.

(b) The job performance scale (Sharma, 1979) was used for data on four dimensions of performance, i.e., the quality and quantity of work, behaviour with peers and with supervisors. The rating was one by two persons—the foreman and the manager. Interjudge reliability of the ratings is 91.

(c) For getting information on the background variables, such as, age, marital status, family income, education, etc., a proforma was used.

Table 6.1 presents the correlation coefficients between the perception of the dimensions of humanization of work and the job performance.

It may be observed that the democracy at the place of work (participation) is positively related to the level of job performance, whereas equity is negatively related to job performance. The equity theory also suggests that if there is inequity there is a behaviour for resolving the equity. This is perhaps the reason for the negative relationship. Individuation also shows a negative relationship. Those who feel that their ability, creativity and other potentials are not getting due development opportunity are trying to compensate that by better work.

TABLE - 6.1
CORRELATION COEFFICIENTS BETWEEN PERCEPTION OF DIMENSIONS OF HUMANIZATION OF WORK AND JOB PERFORMANCE

Security	.061
Equity	.291*
Individuation	.260*
Participation	.397*

*Significant .01 level

In the light of these observations it may be suggested that the humanization of work dimension are important elements for the strategies for job design. The jobs should be designed for people and not just for the sake of work. Since this approach is directed towards concern for feeling of self-worth and human dignity, this is fully congruent with the organizations pragmatic goals and effectiveness in the long run. Therefore the need for human resource policy to integrate the quality of working life concept.

Very closely tied to this is the perception of equity and justice at the place of work. The concept though subjective in nature, is deeply embedded into the human resource policies and work culture of the organizations. In the next few pages an analysis of this process is presented.

Perception of Equity and Justice

Every member of an organization expects equity and justice at the place of work. In fact an ideal and healthy society is characterized by symbols such as 'justice' and 'fairness'. However, often there are no absolute standards of social justice. This is because there are different expectations in the minds of people and there are different cultural norms prevalent in different societies. The analysis of the concept of social justice lies in the cognitive processes. Perceptions of the members of society are the most important components of the phenomenon. Social scientists have so far used various dimensions of this problem at the place of work. In the literature of psychology, topics like dissatisfaction, stress and frustrations have often been linked to the mental state of an individual resulting from the consequence of social injustice. However in the development of Equity Theory, Adam (1965) has presented a comprehensive analysis of the perception and evaluation by the individual as a major basis for human action. The phenomenon of social injustice fits well with this explanation. This is because psychologists assume that interaction among cognitions which have the character of motivational forces trigger behavioural outcomes.

The situations of 'social justice' has two participants i.e., the person (and his perception) and the policy makers manager or the society. This section addresses itself to the micro side of the issue, emphasizing the inequity in perceptions of the participants. The analysis is presented within the framework of Equity Theory (Adam, 1965) which suggests that inequitable perception of job opportunities would lead to stress and dissatisfaction, leading to poor quality of life perception. This might also lead to aggression. Therefore it is possible to explain the agitated behaviour of employees through this psychological perspective. Quality of work, life perceptions of women is yet another example of the perception of social justice and inequity in perception. It is suggested that for development of healthy society/organizations an alternative social policy is needed which would take into consideration the development, the climate of equity for its members. Taking a dynamic perspective of Equity Theory an attempt has been made to explain the concept of justice and women.

Festinger's theory of Social Comparison (1954, A & B) and Cognitive Dissonance, and Trivaut Kelley's (1959) concept of "Comparison level", Stouffer's (1949) principle of 'Relative Deprivation', Merton's (1957) 'Reference group' and Homen's contribution (1961, 1965) of 'Fair Exchange and Distributive Justice' made significant contributions in development of the concept. Even though this conceptualization seems to focus on different aspects of the evaluation process, the basic tenet seems to be moving around the social evaluation concept, which might lead to positive, negative or natural consequences. Taking thread from aforesaid theories, Adam's Equity Theory presents most explicit formulation to understand the underlying motivational dynamics of human behaviour. The variables of this theory are input, outcomes, comparison process, perception of overrewarded or underrewarded, resolution of this feeling and behavioural outcomes.

Inputs are described as attributes a person perceives as his/her contribution to the exchange situation such as his seniority, age, education, skill, experience, intelligence, effort, etc. However, the perception of the contributor is not necessarily isomorphic with the perception of the party in exchange situation. Outcomes refer to the receipts or rewards the person receives like pay, promotion, intrinsic rewards, seniority, etc. Both of these are often correlated and have the characteristics of 'relevance' and 'recognition'. The heart of Equity Theory is the exchange process which always has a person, system, or group as referent; the most common referent being a co-worker. Adams proposed that if there is equity in perception it becomes a source of tension, which is proportional to the magnitude of inequity present. This tension motivates an individual to reduce or eliminate the feeling of inequity. The resolution of inequity takes different forms for different people such as a person might alter his input and his outcome or distort these cognitively. He might change his referent or under extreme circumstance might leave the field. Thus, this theory presents a model of the exchange process, focusing on the individual's attitudinal and behavioural reactions of perceived injustice. As already emphasized this is a cognitive model of motivation, which conceives a person as an information processing system. In this information processing the characteristics of the person, the situation and the information, all are equally important, Wyer (1974).

The occupational choices of women are also governed by the aforesaid factors, i.e., their own characteristics including education, the job climate of our country and the relevant information about various types of jobs and government policies that the person is exposed to. Super and Bohn (1970) postulate that career choice and development are essentially a process of synthesis of the person's self-concept with the realities of external environment. However, one may be dismayed in the process of the implementation of one's self-concept and reality testing. As the equity theory explains, they find that in spite of good education and other qualities they are unable to get a job of their choice. It is, however, possible to neutralize this situation. In other words, make it more equitable if by close look to the input/outcome/ referent characteristics. First of all, the situation has to be analyzed from development perspective. The ultimate motivator for human adults according to Schein (1983) can be thought of as the need to maintain and develop one's self-concept and one's self-esteem. Further, one of the implications of developmental theory is that the pattern of the choice behaviour is largely determined from childhood reinforces to patterns of need, values and motives. These inputs and other opportunities in comparison to referents create a situation of inequity for many women employees in India. While most of them consider this as a situation of social injustice. First of all there are certain groups in our society who have been experiencing inequity because of lack of opportunities, poverty and some such factors.

Working women group fall in several categories, i.e., women engaged in domestic duties only, women in labour force, in teaching profession, in offices and in managerial/ administrative positions as discussed earlier in this book. The highest inequity perception group perhaps is the group of women engaged in domestic duties playing important supportive functions for other earning members of the family. Often household work and child bearing are considered as valueless. We forget that no nation can make a mark unless the children of that nation are healthy. For doing this noble work, the society is impinging, such social injustice to women 'consciously' or 'unconsciously'. The lot of working women are also quite similar. One often finds that employers' hesitation in keeping women employees for various social reasons and there is job insecurity and exploitation. Women often find that in comparison to their male colleagues they get late promotions, lesser salaries and poorer benefits.

Therefore there is an urgent need to give special training to women workers, remove their drudgery, and impart diversity training as part of human resource policy to improve attitude towards them and provide them equal occupational status in practice.

Much has been said, written and analyzed on the subject of working women. Yet, despite a greater worldwide focus of attention on them, working women continue to be clogged by innumerable problems. Our constitution assures and seeks to ensure equality for all its citizens, irrespective of sex, propounding the concept that men and women are equal. Yet, the concept of "equal opportunity in employment", needs to be reviewed in the context of the diversity in women's life situations, in different social segments, for certain classes, employment is viewed as a "survival strategy", while for some it is a "factor of mobility". On the broad spectrum of women's employment at one end are women as casual labour in the most strenuous industries in unskilled and low paid jobs, and at the other end are high status professional women workers. The latter create an illusion about ideas like "individual merit". But, the majority of women are handicapped by their illiteracy, lack of training and a host of psycho-social pressures, the principle of equality of opportunity remains inoperative. Thus, this principle has remained an abstract one, in a society characterized by social and economic inequalities.

As discussed above, women's work includes both unremunerative and remunerative (or paid) work. The former includes all life support activities and the contents differ with class, age, and residence (rural/urban). It covers unpaid work of women on family farms, enterprises, etc. This component is neither valued nor counted by most of the official data system, and has remained a grey area of research. An ILO report estimating the values of "housework" says that women contribute roughly 25-39% of the GNP.

With regard to job-related issues (i.e. inadequate representation of women in skilled and managerial posts, short-term commitment of women to the labour force, women preference to work at home, or their preference for certain kind of jobs, etc.), some of the explanations are presented below.

Many analysts argue that women's family responsibilities account for their unique positions in the workplace. Research suggests that the socialization, deficiencies and structural institutionalization of female stress types affects their preparation for future life. Family obligations have different meanings for boys and girls. The discrimination to which girls are subjected at home is clearly reflected in the job market where employees have jobs "suitable" for women.

Role differentiation theory stresses that women and men are likely that women option differently because of differences in work patterns and roles in the family. This gives rise to blatant, forms of discrimination based on marital status.

About 80% working women are engaged in agriculture and allied activities, 94% work in the unorganised or informal sector in low paid, low skilled and unsecured jobs. Due to the lack of education, training resources and productive assets, economic recession, mechanization and automation throws them out of employment. The decline of women's employment in traditional industries, i.e., mines, textile, tobacco, handicrafts, has not been compensated by the expansion of opportunities for women.

With the new wave of attention on women's issues, people seem to advocate a job and financial security as the ultimate to secure independence and happiness for women. Where financial means are no doubt necessary to satisfy every human being lower order needs and allows him/her to strive for self-esteem and dignity, the path of achieving them, for women, is fraught with ills, problems and even greater exploitation simply because they work.

Finding a suitable occupation is the first problem. Involving her rights and wish to do so proceeds it, and of course fighting for the right amount of education to secure a decent job tops it all. After having completed her education when a woman steps into her chosen field, she experiences that people's attitudes to working women are not quite encouraging or correct.

Finally, we attempt to find out perception of equity among working women in terms of their salaries. Tables 6.2 and 6.3 present the percentages of working women and men of different age groups. In the age group of 26-30 years, 5.6% women expect very high salary whereas only 3.5% men expect that. Perception of inequity increases in the working women group, highest being in the age group of 40-50 years (18.9%). Among men of this age group only 8.8% say that they should get more salary than what they are getting.

In this study of 147 professional men and women regarding their perception by salary it is observed that 53.3% women and 57.9% men feel that they should get more salary than what they are presently getting. However, 14.4% women expect very high salary. But among men only 10.5% expect very high salary. This clearly indicated that there is greater inequity among women professionals in terms of salary they earn.

Thus, one begins to see how the concept of "equality of opportunities" becomes meaningless in an unequal class, caste and gender matrix. Any move towards improving the lot of the working women cannot be feasible without acknowledging her family into account, her historical disadvantages position due to centuries of male domination and internationalized values about her self worth, roles and priorities, unequal education, professional training and property rights, as well as her reproductive role, which requires support for child case, extended leave, retraining and re-entry.

Even though the responsibility of developing the climate of "social justice" lies with every member of organization, the policy makers, teachers and family also have a major responsibility, as it basically means development of social justice in a healthy society through inculcation of positive attitudes at home and school/ college and organization.

TABLE - 6.2

SALARY AND EQUITY PERCEPTION OF WORKING WOMEN IN DIFFERENT AGE GROUPS (PERCENTAGE)

Age Group	You should get				
	Less salary thanwhat you are getting	*Just what you are getting*	*More salary than what you are getting*	*Very high salary than what they are getting*	*Total*
26-30	-	(10)	(4.4)	(5.6)	(20)
30-40	-	(8.9)	(16.7)	(4.4)	(28.9)
40-50	(2.2)	(4.4)	(18.9)	(2.2)	(27.8)
Above 50	-	(4.4)	(8.9)	-	(13.3)
X	(1.1)	(1.1)	(5.6)	(2.2)	(10)
	(3.3)	(28.9)	(53.3)	(14.4)	90(100)

TABLE - 6.3

SALARY AND EQUITY PERCEPTION OF MEN IN DIFFERENT AGE GROUPS (PERCENTAGES)

Age Group	You should get				
	Less salary thanwhat you are getting	*Just what you are getting*	*More salary than what you are getting*	*Very high salary than what they are getting*	*Total*
Below 26	(1.8)	(8.8)	(14)	-	(24.6)
26-30	(3.5)	(10.5)	(14)	(3.5)	(31.6)
30-40	-	(1.8)	(14)	(5.3)	(21)
40-50	-	(3.5)	(8.8)	(1.8)	(14)
Above 50	-	(1.8)	(7)	-	(8.8)
X	-	-	-	-	0(0)
	(5.3)	(26.3)	(57.9)	(10.5)	57(100)

SEVEN

Some Reflections on Human Resource Policies and Women

Human resource policies generally include selection, training, performance appraisals, career development, motivational strategies, reward and compensation along with job analysis and team performance evaluation. An attempt has been made here to analyse these factors in industries and how motivational strategies and reward and compensation are perceived by male and female employees.

The human resource policies in many Indian organizations still remain at the welfare management and personal management stages, without any emphasis to the process oriented work culture and evaluation. As a result of this, new techniques of selection and performance appraisal are rare and often training programmes are at a level of ritual rather than a serious pursuit. For many organizations any investment in training programmes and related activities have not come to a stage of serious budget allocations. This may be partly due to the intangible gains of such efforts. Women are the biggest sufferers because of such managerial attitudes.

In India, women are burdened with cumulative inequalities as a result of socio-cultural and economic discriminatory practices, which have been taken for granted.

However, one of the most significant developments in the post-independent India is the speed with which women have successfully challenged men in various walks of life, particularly in formal organizations. This has badly hurt the psyche of the Indian male too.

A close look at the reasons of secondary status of women reveals that the economic dependence of women upon men has played a pivotal role. Now that an increasing number of women are going in for formal education and full-time employment the situation is fast changing.

In a study of women workers of Kanpur, Sharma (1996) presented the following three major dimensions of the working conditions of the women workers:

1. Recruitment procedure adopted by employers to women workers.
2. Objective working conditions like:
   (a) wages
   (b) benefits in terms of leave, bonus, insurance, etc.
   (c) promotional prospects
   (d) stability in jobs
   (e) relationship with superiors or bosses
   (f) physical work environment
3. Job satisfaction and commitment

Here the women workers' attitude to present job, their awareness of exploitation at the workplace and willingness to continue their present professional career have been studied separately. Figures 7.1 to 7.7 present the analysis in the following pages

Recruitment

The recruitment procedure for hiring women workers in the industrial and non-industrial units of public and private sectors make an interesting as well as revealing comparison.

The recruitment methods prevalent in the public and private sectors as reported by the respondents have been presented in the form of pie-charts in Figure 7.1.

To sum up, the following four factors seem to influence the recruitment of women workers more commonly in Kanpur and in that order:

(a) Personal influence of friends and relatives.
(b) Humanitarian considerations for either wards or widows of the dead employees.
(c) Primordial considerations or regional or linguistic ties caste or kinship.
(d) On merits.

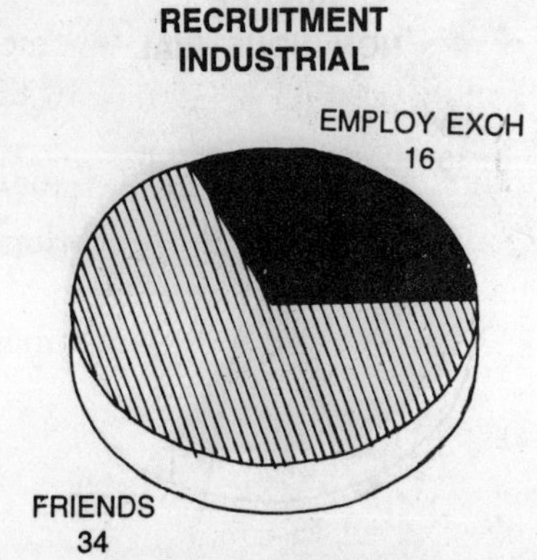

PRIVATE SECTOR

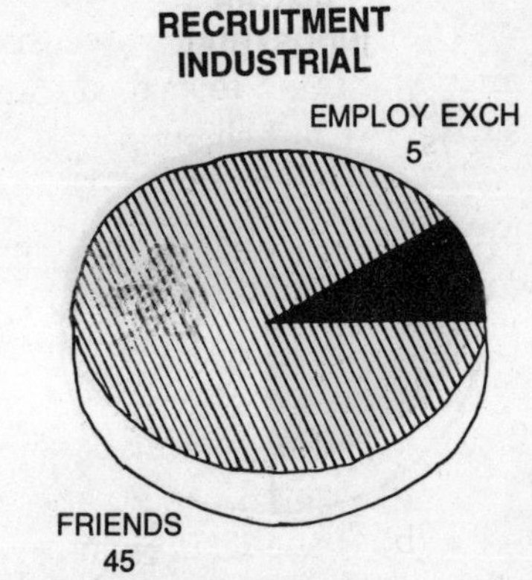

PUBLIC SECTOR

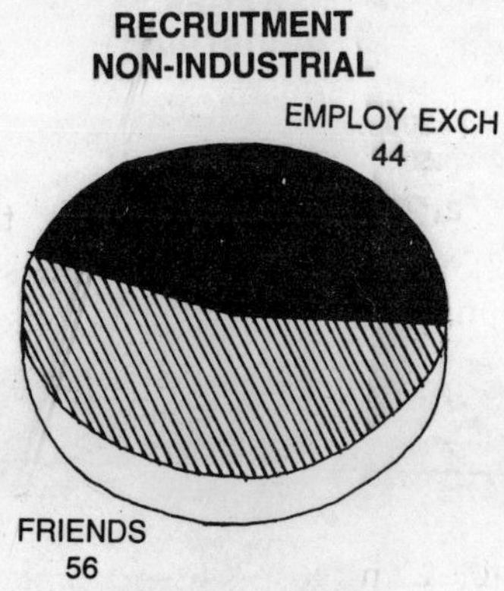

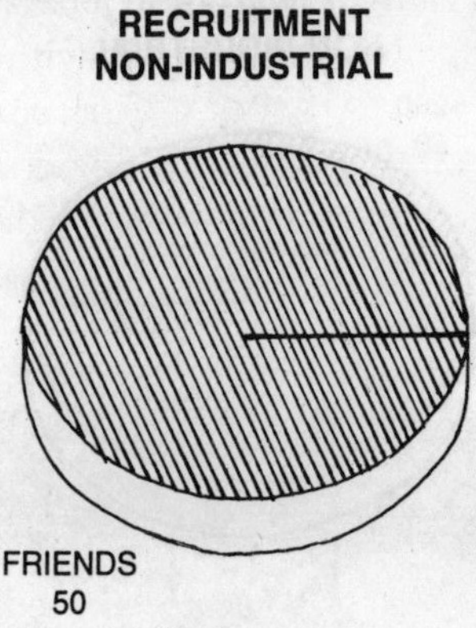

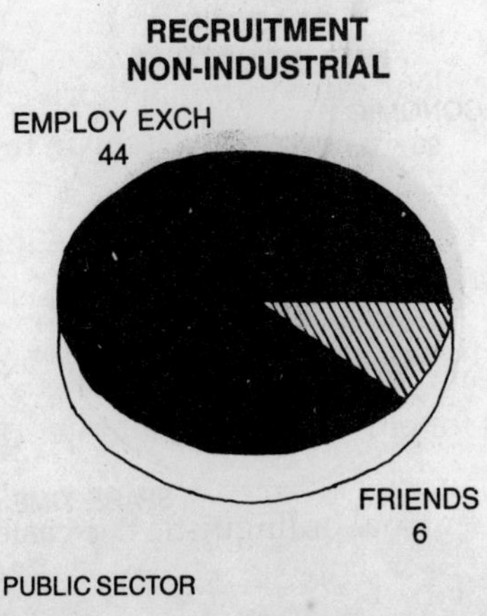

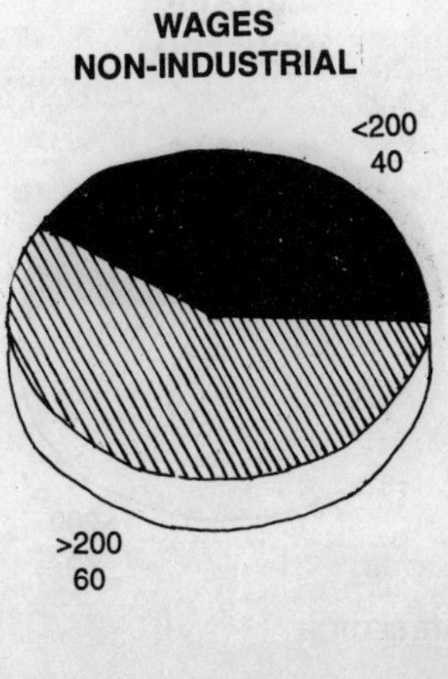

PUBLIC SECTOR

WAGES INDUSTRIAL

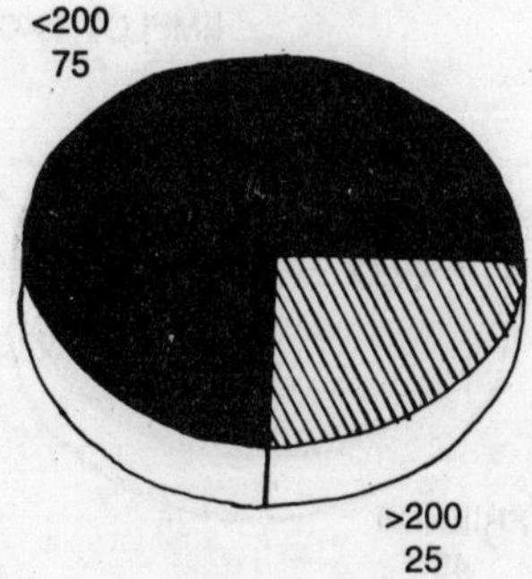

WAGES NON-INDUSTRIAL

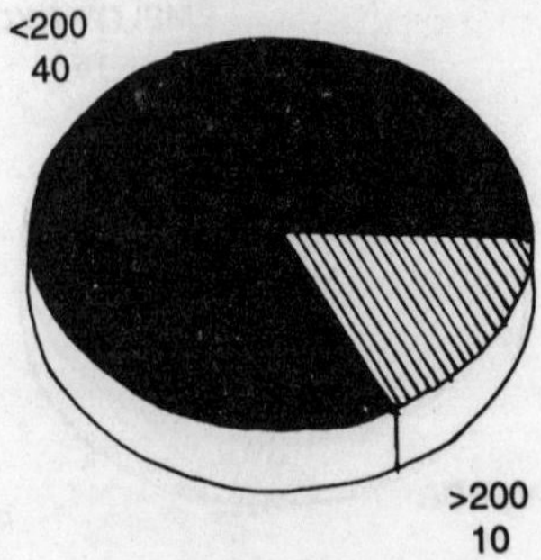

PRIVATE SECTOR

WAGES NON-INDUSTRIAL

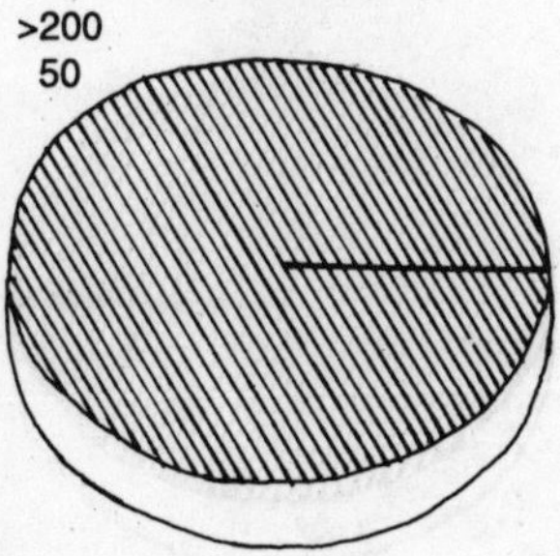

PUBLIC SECTOR

WAGES INDUSTRIAL

PRIVATE SECTOR

WAGES INDUSTRIAL

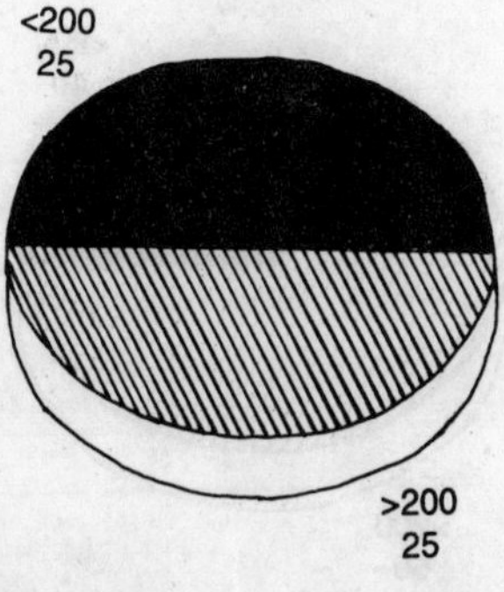

PRIVATE SECTOR

REASONS NON-INDUSTRIAL

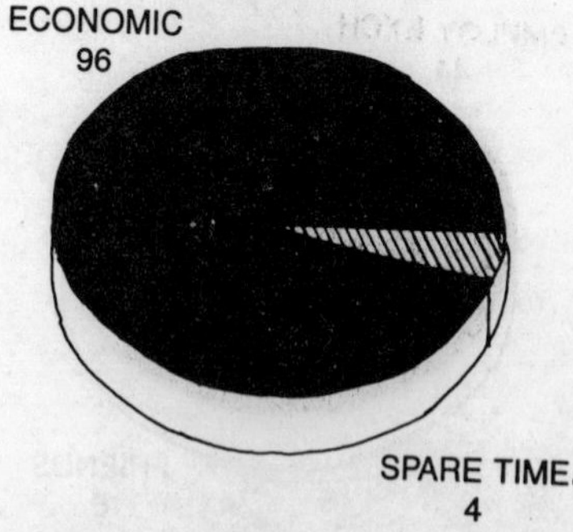

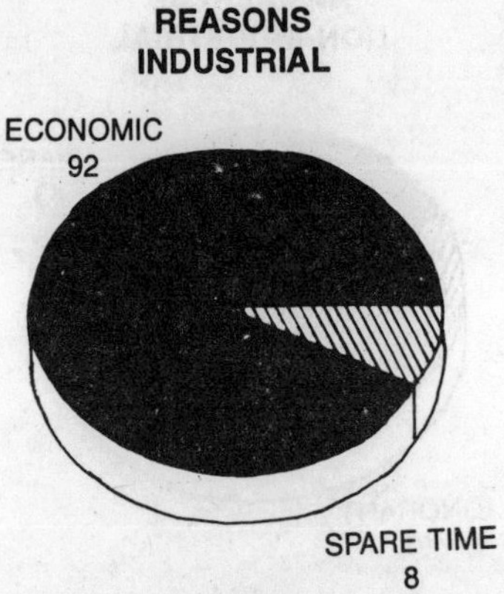
REASONS
INDUSTRIAL
ECONOMIC
92
SPARE TIME
8

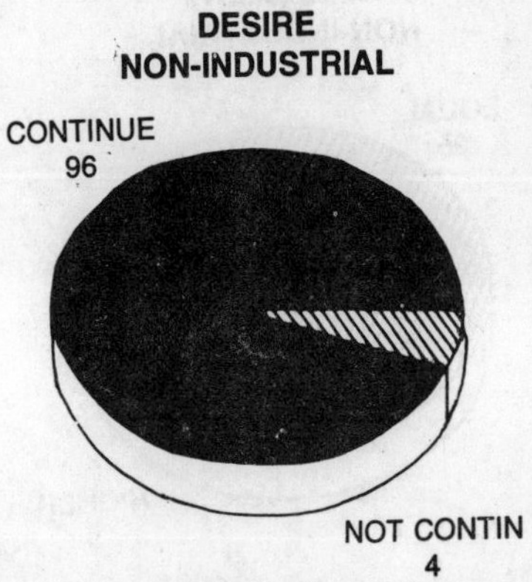
DESIRE
NON-INDUSTRIAL
CONTINUE
96
NOT CONTIN
4

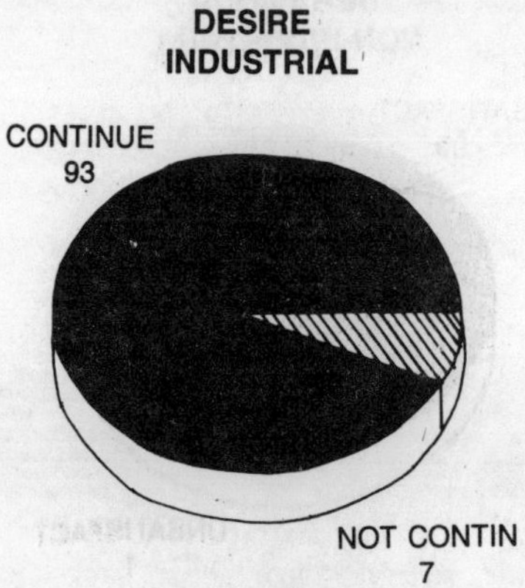
DESIRE
INDUSTRIAL
CONTINUE
93
NOT CONTIN
7

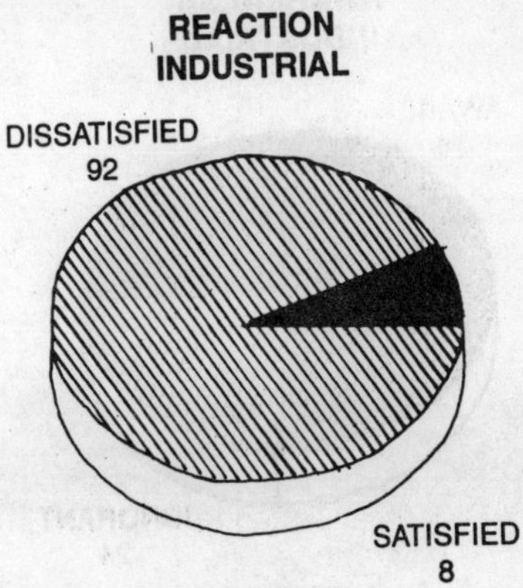
REACTION
INDUSTRIAL
DISSATISFIED
92
SATISFIED
8

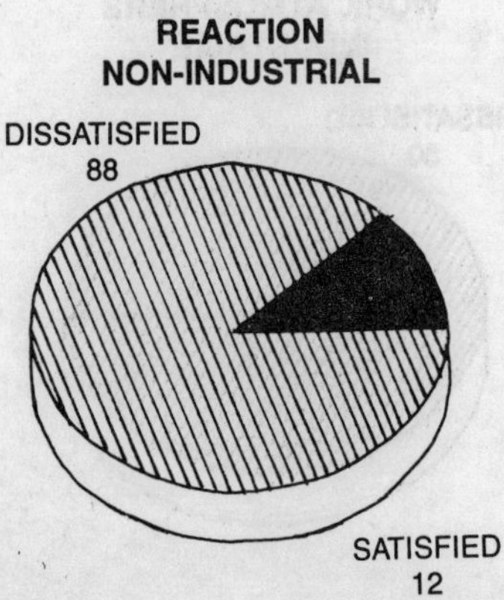
REACTION
NON-INDUSTRIAL
DISSATISFIED
88
SATISFIED
12

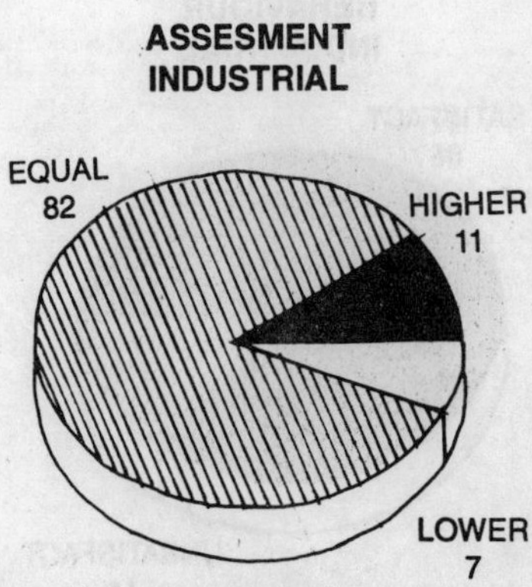
ASSESMENT
INDUSTRIAL
EQUAL
82
HIGHER
11
LOWER
7

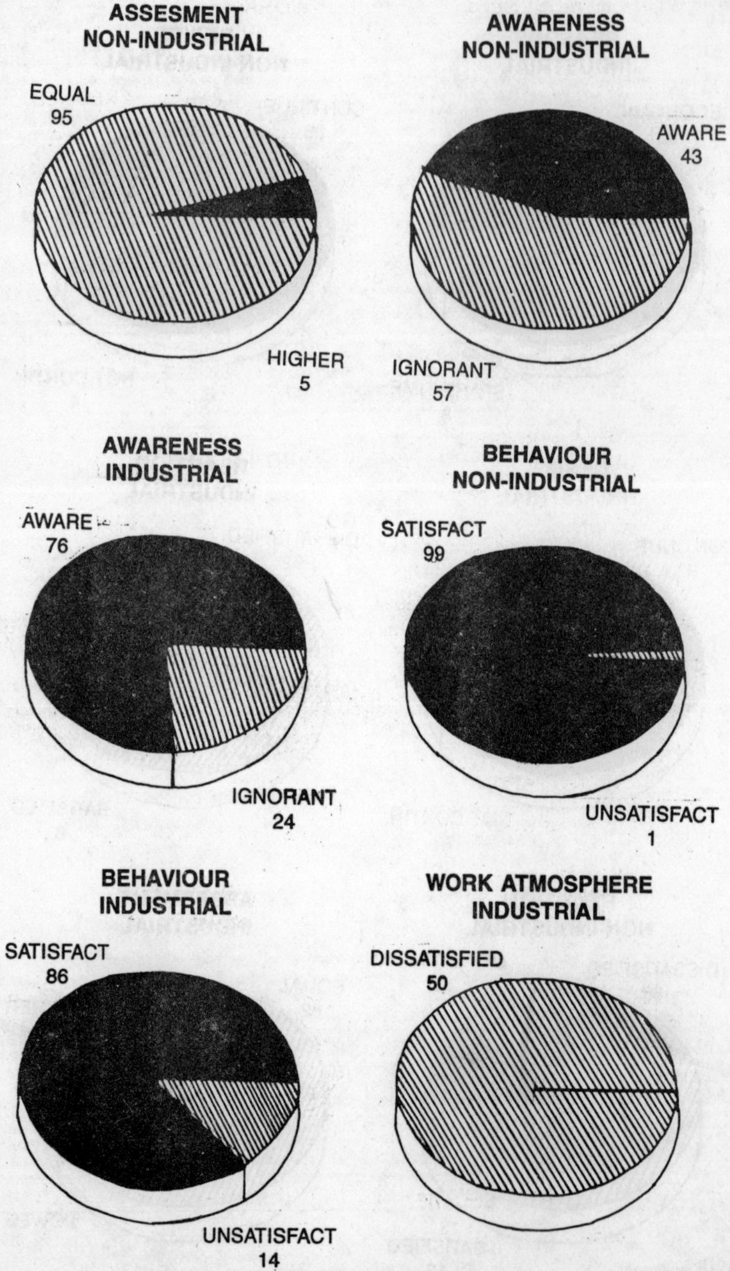

PUBLIC SECTOR

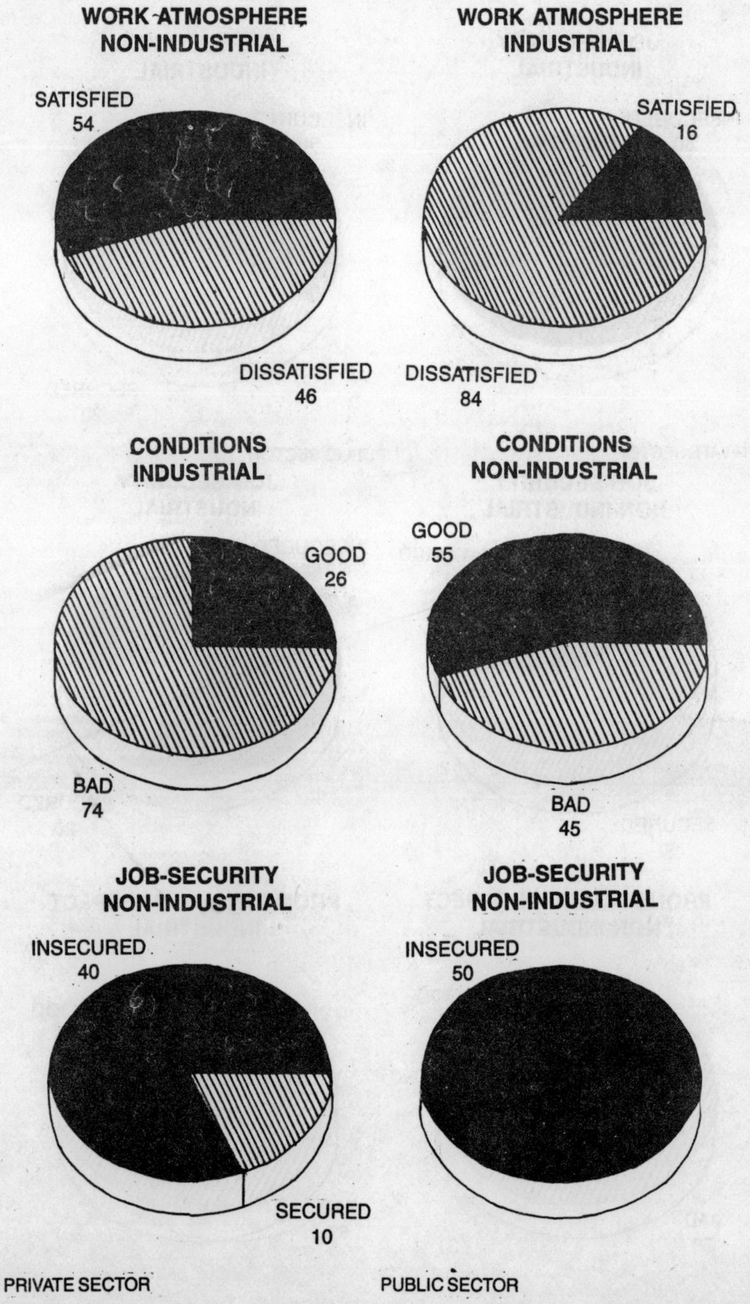
WORK ATMOSPHERE
NON-INDUSTRIAL
SATISFIED
54
DISSATISFIED
46
WORK ATMOSPHERE
INDUSTRIAL
SATISFIED
16
DISSATISFIED
84
CONDITIONS
INDUSTRIAL
GOOD
26
BAD
74
CONDITIONS
NON-INDUSTRIAL
GOOD
55
BAD
45
JOB-SECURITY
NON-INDUSTRIAL
INSECURED
40
SECURED
10
JOB-SECURITY
NON-INDUSTRIAL
INSECURED
50
PRIVATE SECTOR
PUBLIC SECTOR

JOB-SECURITY
INDUSTRIAL

JOB-SECURITY
INDUSTRIAL

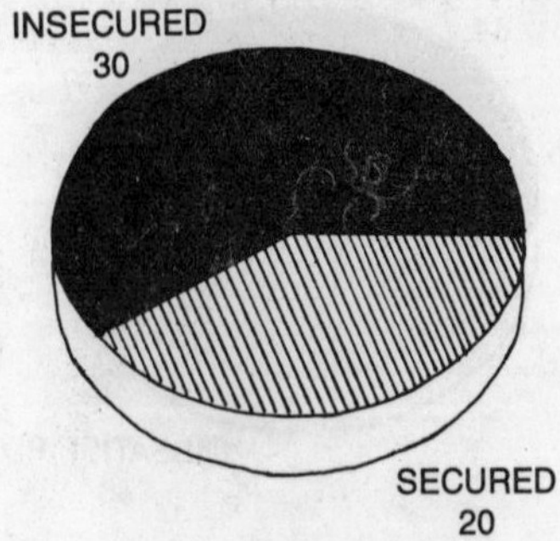

PRIVATE SECTOR

PUBLIC SECTOR

JOB-SECURITY
NON-INDUSTRIAL

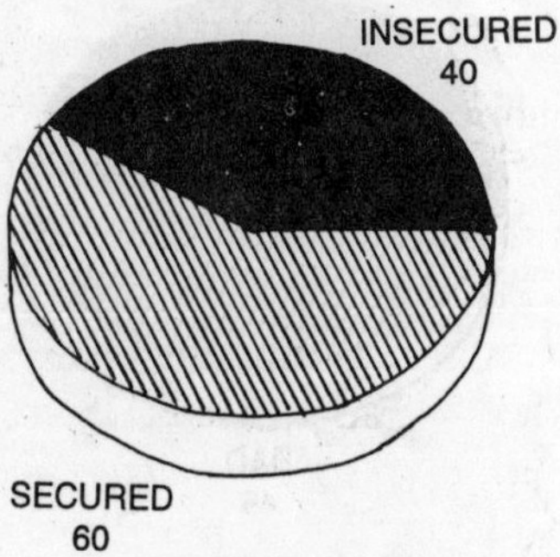

JOB-SECURITY
INDUSTRIAL

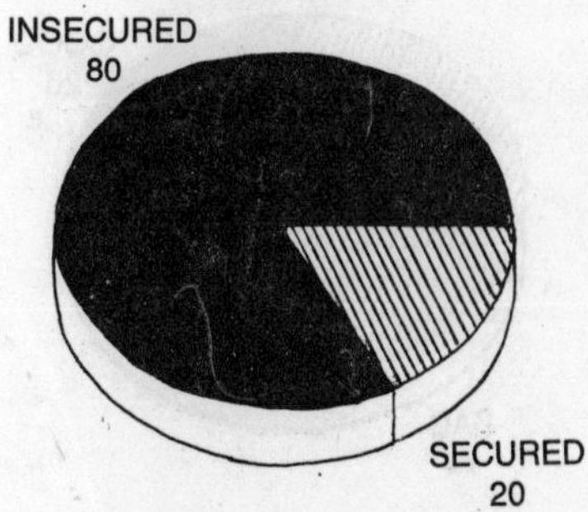

PROMOTIONAL PROSPECT
NON-INDUSTRIAL

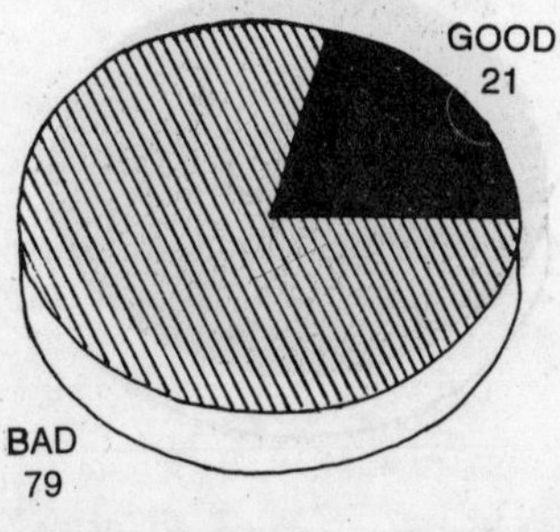

PROMOTIONAL PROSPECT
INDUSTRIAL

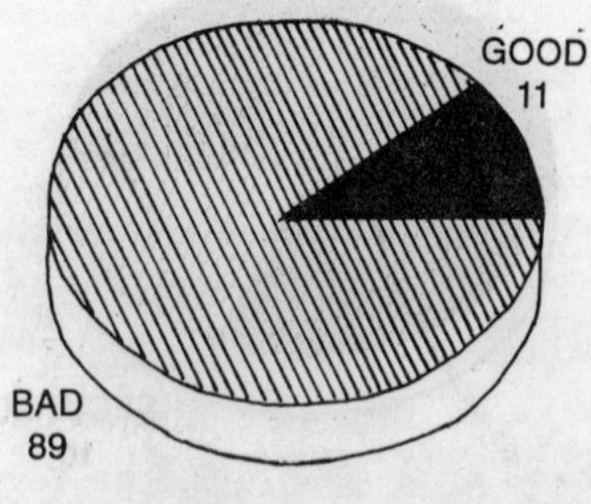

Wages

Difference in wages received by the respondents from the public and private sector units have been presented in the form of pie-charts in Figure 7.2. It shows that a large percentage of women workers got very low wages.

Benefits

As far as benefits were concerned it was observed that women workers did not get any benefit like earned leave, medical or maternity care, etc. In theory they are always entitled to these benefits but seldom get them in reality.

If wages and benefits received are taken as reliable indicators of the working conditions then there cannot be two opinions that the working conditions of the women workers in Kanpur are deplorable and poor.

Job Security

For job security among the industrial and non-industrial respondents working in the public and private sector units see pie-charts in Figure 7.6.

Promotion Prospects

For promotion prospects as perceived by the respondents see pie-charts in Figure 7.7.

Based on this information it can be said that most of the women workers never got promotion in their jobs nor subjectively perceive promotion prospects in the near future.

Physical Atmosphere at Workplace

Respondents' reaction to the work atmosphere in the industrial and non-industrial units of public and private sectors have been presented in the form of pie-charts.

The main reason for dissatisfaction was the fact that their work duration almost always exceeded 8 hours a day. Other reasons includes uncushioned stools, stuffy rooms, etc.

Social Relationship with the Supervisors

Assessment of the Conditions

Findings revealed that those units where women workers were better organized and effectively participated in their trade union activities, invariably reported better working conditions.

That the working conditions of women workers objectively speaking were quite bad in terms of recruitment procedure, wages, benefits, jobs security, etc., can hardly be disputed. But the question to be answered is that do the women workers have subjective awareness of their exploitation by their managements or employers. Do they know they have been and are being exploited by their bosses?

Figures show that a majority of the non-industrial women workers did not perceive their exploitation as compared to industrial female employees. This marked difference in the perception of exploitation between industrial and non-industrial women workers also partly explains the difference in their participation in trade-union activities. Hence there exists a positive association between the trade-union participation and the subjective awareness of exploitation.

Job Satisfaction and Commitment

The study dwells into the main aspects of job commitment seen in:

(i) their attitude towards the present job.

(ii) their attitude towards pursuing their present careers/ occupations.

The data shows that women workers generally do not develop a strong attachment to their jobs. This is due to the fact that the jobs to which women workers have access involve routine, monotonous and low paid work with little or no future prospects.

The women workers' keenness to pursue their occupational careers despite their present jobs is quite noteworthy and this commitment is mainly born out of economic necessity.

Motivation for Money

Values are the foundation for understanding motivation and attitudes of people and their work playing important role in the study of human resources. Values also influence perception of people and as a result of that, certain outcomes or situations are preferred. Most important source of values come from the socialization process and the environment. Parents, teachers, neighbourhood, school, clubs, television and movies and overall reinforcement of certain behaviour are the major contributing factors. Also values are relatively stable and have close linkage with ethical behaviour. An analysis of value based attitudes for men and women from India is presented here.

Every employee has a crystallized and complex set of needs, values, way of perceiving the world and his personality which he brings with him to his workplace. He is, thus, not a raw mould. He tries to fit his psychological make-up with the climate of the organization. The fact, that his psychological characteristics influence his behaviour, suggests that his job behaviour and motivation for job performance will also be influenced by these characteristics. This means that in hiring a worker one always hires the whole man and performance and output of the organization depends on summation of these characteristics, particularly values and perception of its members.

The managerial experts of organizations are trying hard to understand the new workforce and turning to the field of human behaviour to gain insights into their job perception and related performance. Behavioural science revolution has more recently also focused upon man's needs and values fostering better performance so as to maximize both human satisfaction and productivity.

In general, productivity of an organization depends upon two major variables, employee's job performance and technological factors including equipment, method, job design and raw materials. Disregarding technological considerations, the job performance of the worker depends primarily on employee's ability and motivation to perform. The ability generally depends upon skill, job knowledge and factors like intelligence, but the motivational aspect of the individual job performance is a much more complex phenomenon.

Human performance of almost any sort can be improved by increase in motivation and it is viewed that job performance is a function of skill level multiplied by motivation. Vroom (1964) also emphasized that job performance is a result of interaction among worker's skill, ability and motivation.

According to Sutemeister (1963), if a person had no motivation, he could be the most capable individual in the world, but there would be no relationship between his ability and job performance. Thus, both, ability and motivation, are essential aspects of the job and individual needs, some forces may act as positive and contribute to motivation, improving job performance of some employees, whereas to others, these may be neutral or even negative reducing employee motivation, resulting in poor performance. What actually happens to employee's performance which depends on the strength of multidimensional centripedal and centrifugal forces, which may be within the job, worker himself or within the organization.

Individual's values, attitudes, habits and beliefs act as a steering system to motivation process affecting the job performance. Work which has become highly complex phenomenon with present technological changes and developments, may be perceived as a task, a duty or an accomplishment, drudgery or even play. It could give intrinsic satisfaction to some and could be drudgery to others. Regardless of its meaning "work" or "job" cannot be considered apart from the individual who performs it. Therefore his motives, social interaction and personality must be taken into account to arrive at a conclusion why with the similar ability some persons are more effective in the industry than others. Industries have generally overlooked the complexities of human motivation and have tried to oversimplify this by introducing incentives to sustain worker motivation. Therefore, there is an urgent need to consider this issue, where individual differences play an important role. Under Indian conditions, where we have taken to industrialization in a big way, this is a much more challenging question. Insights into this problem might help us to develop new design of work and make effective systems.

Values play an important role in motivating employees. However, the dynamics of values for money are much more complex than normally assumed to be. According to psychologists money could be an anxiety reducer, a gauge of success, a primary survival motivation or a power to buy or dominate. The behavioural outcomes related to money depend on individual perception and personality.

The main objective behind this section is to present the extent of value orientation of people. To analyze the 'work-money' perception dynamics we have categorized this field-study into the following main issues:

- Pay (from the job) as a motivator.
- Desire to get additional money (apart from the usual pay).
- Preference of money over certain other types of facilities and incentives at the place of work.

The Study

The sample covered under the study includes a total of four hundred and fifty-eight respondents who are working in private sector organizations in India. Table 7.1 presents the details.

The procedure of data collection has been primarily a structured questionnaire with questions, divided into three main sub-groups as mentioned earlier.

TABLE - 7.1
DESCRIPTION OF SAMPLE

Working and Non-Working Men/Women	*Per cent*
Working Men	35.6
Non-Working Men (Students)	26.7
Working Women	13.3
Non-Working Women	24.4
	100.0
N = 458	

The first section analyzes the pay (money) from job as motivator as compared to:

Job security;
Good working conditions;
Promotion;
Autonomy and independence;
Authority and power associated with the job; and
earning self-respect and dignity;

The analysis reveals the following:

- In general, the total sample has ranked, earning self-respect/ dignity, i.e., fulfilling the self-esteem motive (Maslow's hierarchy of needs) as the most important motivating factor, followed by good working conditions.

- The working sample of our study primarily includes employees of private companies hence no preference to job security over pay from the job.
- The working sample has given preference to authority, power, autonomy and independence as compared to the non-working sample.

The second issue relates to values embedded into people's desire to get money (apart from their usual pay), i.e., to what extent can people go for the extraneous money the statements are related to the actions respondents would like to take in getting more/extra money.

The choices are as follows:

(i) Undertaking more responsibility for more money
(ii) Doing illegal work for more money
(iii) Raising the quality of work for more money
(iv) Raising the quantity of work for more money
(v) Working for extra hours or spending less time with family for earning more money
(vi) Prefer highly paying job, although job is non-challenging.

Analysis of this part reveals that:

(a) Samples of Working respondents have not agreed to the statement that they would raise their quality to work for more money as the non-working have done.
(b) Working respondents have agreed to take more responsibility for more money while non-working have agreed very strongly to this idea.
(c) Working respondents have objected to the idea of leaving their present job without knowing any thing about the new job, while non-working responders have supported it.
(d) Samples of Working respondents have not agreed to spend less time with family for more money while non-working have generally supported the idea.

The third issue raised performance of money over certain other work conditions:

(i) Working in a small organization paying more money.
(ii) Working in a big, famous organization paying less money.
(iii) Working in an organization that gives less money but brings out creative talents.

(iv) Social-service type of job, as compared to high paying job.

(v) Research job as compared to high paying job.

(vi) A teaching and educational job as compared to a high paying marketing job.

Analysis reveals interesting results:

(a) Working category has strongly agreed to accept a job that brings out creative talents as compared to non-working respondents who don't give high preference to creativity.

(b) Overall sample has opted for a job bringing out creative abilities as the first choice over a high paying job in a big famous organization.

In the first issue, money refers to the fixed pay from the job, since this is generally fixed the respondents have opted for other parameters, viz., job security, promotion, working conditions, etc., over money because these motivating factors are under their control and define their values, roles and behaviour in the organization.

The second category of money refers to a value-based concept. The study has shown that large number of respondents are ready to raise the quality and quantity of their work for more money.

The third category of questions clearly reflects that the overall sample has preferred money (high paying job) over a social service, research and development and a teaching/educational job.

It is important to mention that although the working sample chosen for the study includes people from different organizations, but the non-working sample primarily includes the students that may be sharing similar views due to common value systems of a highly prestigious institute. Hence we believe that a larger and more diversified sample could have strongly aided us in proving our points.

"Man does not live by bread alone ....," so the Bible says. A lot of businessmen today are adding, "Nor does he work for bread alone, at least not any more". This is because power and achievement motivation are also reflected in having more money.

There is a growing realization that the employee today is indeed, a new breed, he appears to have different values, needs, motivations than his predecessor.

Motivation, that ubiquitous theme in contemporary

management literature, seems to be the prime concern of the manager, who is trying not just to turn out a product, but to gain a competitive edge in the market place.

The concept of money as a value and motivation (i.e. what motivates people to work) evolved way back in late nineteenth century when the theorists supporting 'Scientific Management' school suggested that money is the prime motivator for the workforce. It was later realized by the 'Behavioural Science' experts that innumerable number of other social, psychological, social-psychological factors also contribute to work motivation. The factors of job security among women studied here like autonomy, authority and power, promotion and money forming the motivational force give clear reflections on the significance of diversity movement and the human resource policy for India and suggest that women's perception of money is different than that of men.

EIGHT

Human Resource Management and Women: Looking Ahead

In the scientific studies of Human Resource Management there are various models suggesting reshaping of employment relationships and a great deal of change because of contingent issues. As we have presented in this book that there is no single coherent theory of Human Resource Management particularly with reference to 'women at work'. This is because Human Resource Management is an ongoing process and system-oriented concept embedded in the social system. The input and outcome of human potentials, experience and emphasis of satisfaction and performance are some key issues. However, there are a number of explanations, i.e., developmental, strategic, restatement and fusion (Beardwell and Holden, 1994) in terms of Human Resource Management. Management of cultural change, modernity of attitudes, aspirations exceptions, changing personal and social values, perceptions, changing need for empowerment, fairness and awareness about world and many such issues impinge on the Human Resource Management issues and affect the women — the new workforce of the next millennium. However, gender has been 'mis- or under-represented' in organization theory (Calas and Smircich, 1992) and hegemony is seen the way gender 'issues are emphasized in the organization theories (Hearn, 1989). In this context Marshall (1982) argued the feminist thinking challenges traditional knowledge which has been largely constructed about men and by men, devaluating and ignoring experiences of women. This phenomenon is common all over the globe. However, in India it is fast developing as a new social order which is called modernization by many thinkers. Figure 8.I presents a model of social change and modernity. This suggests that a multivariate continuous phenomenon there is need to be proactive. Organizations need to bring about human resource policy changes to give women equal opportunities and suitable work culture.

Economic Factors	Employment Opportunities			
Psychological Factors	Aspiration and Expectation of Women	Changes in values and attitudes	Changes in roles and structures	Moderni-zation
Social Factors	Educational Opportunities			

Figure 8.1: A Model of Social Change and Modernity

Action Programmes

Some action programmes that show results can and should be initiated by organizations and by women themselves. These could be developmental, attitudinal, strategic or social. Essential for the success of any action programme is an understanding of how women in organization compare with men in the level of jobs. The idea of a working woman is a gift of the modern age. The change is slow but perceptible (Table 8.2). Gradually, with changing social norms the Indian woman is coming out of her home and her traditional role of housewife is shifting towards being an equal partner in family life. The change has been brought by the spread of education Table 8.1 and by the disintegration of the joint family structure. Thus, we are moving, though slowly, but surely towards a new social order in which men and women both contribute, economically towards the well-being of their families and on the whole, to the nation.

In India not many women are able to find jobs suited to their talents and qualifications even though there is significant change in the recent years. Transfer of their husbands in many cases, seriously affects their careers.

TABLE- 8.1
PROGRESS OF LITERACY IN DELHI

Year	*Total Population*	*Literate Persons*		
		Male	*Female*	*Total*
1	2	3	4	5
1931	636246	73377 (19.86)	16095 (6.03)	89472 (14.06)
1941	917939	171233 (31.99)	58370 (15.25)	229603 (25.01)
1951	1744072	424118 (42.99)	244955 (32.34)	669073 (38.36)
1961	2658612	904801 (60.75)	497497 (42.55)	1402298 (52.75)
1971	4065698	1438268 (63.71)	863337 (47.75)	2301605 (56.61)
1981	6220406	2352883 (68.40)	1475443 (53.07)	3828326 (61.54)
1991	9420644	3539500 (82.01)	2342797 (66.99)	5882297 (75.29)

Note: Figures given in parenthesis are percentages.
* Excluding population of 0-6 age group.
Source: Directorate of Census Operations, Delhi.

TABLE - 8.2
LABOUR AND EMPLOYMENT: SCHEDULED CASTES, SCHEDULED TRIBES & PHYSICALLY HANDICAPPED PERSONS ON THE LIVE REGISTER OF THE EMPLOYMENT EXCHANGES IN DELHI

Year	*1971*	*1981*	*1989*	*1990*	*1991*	*1992*	*1993*
1	2	3	4	5	6	7	8
Men	119043	215576	634124	671041	711146	7113306	711035
Women	20177	76412	159492	172284	179740	193686	197000

Source: Directorate of Employment Govt. of National Capital Territory of Delhi.

Working woman is relatively a new phenomenon in our country. The advent of women into offices, industries, schools, hospitals and the like has brought with it complex psychological and sociological problems too. Several questions concerning the course of and the result of these problems have to be faced and solved by the organizations. In the earlier part of the book we have attempted to find out what are the reasons which prompt women to seek work and employment, the kind of jobs that women prefer, the problems that working women face, both at home and at workplace, problems women have in dealing with males colleagues, problems of men in dealing with working women at their workplace and working wives at home and the society's reactions towards working women.

Some of the most visible effects are absence at meal times, inability to cater to the demands of her family and failure to maintain an orderly home, becoming more independent and expectation of share household work, and some readjustment of power relationships at home.

A woman prime minister, Indira Gandhi, along with her long tenure at the helm of the nation's affairs, has inspired the women from all walks of life. The United Nations centred International Women's Year around the following themes representing goals for women.

(a) promotion of equal rights.
(b) integration of women in development
(c) and women's role in strengthening peace

All of these relate to 'women and work'.

Civil Service, traditionally considered to be a man's domain has been invaded by women. In professional fields too (medical, engineering, designing) women have achieved great distinctions. In the last few years women from traditional families are coming forward and taking up initiatives in family business. However, this does not mean that we have achieved our targets. Due to decrease in the number of cottage industries one major source of employment for women has disappeared.

The endeavour of our society should be to achieve what some other countries have done, i.e., making every person a member of country's workforce. This will ensure equality between sexes and also population control. The moment women become an integral part of the workforce and they are accepted as co-workers the work culture will change.

Any such policies related to women workers can however only be implemented through government support like better education for women, equal rights and opportunities and punishments for offenders committing crime against women on the one hand and changing attitudes and work culture of organizations.

Such improvement would lead to successful tapping of human resources in India. The role of women in the workplace has also undergone a major change in the recent years in India. Large number of the employed women are nurses, teachers, social workers, clerks and librarians. There has been a sudden spurt into other fields too, like doctors, lecturers, computer professionals, scientists and engineers.

In addition to the myths discussed earlier there is an assumption that men are preferred for jobs which are strenuous, mobile or intellectual, while women are preferred for jobs which are precise, delicate or repetitive. Such distinctions however, are based on attitudes rather than truth. We have also seen that the occupational careers of women are not normally continuous because of social and child bearing reasons. This gives men greater opportunities.

Even though attention to broadening and improving job opportunities for women is being paid many laws which were passed for all organizations regarding obligations of employees towards women and minorities have not worked effectively. Dynamic interaction among a host of social, economic and technological forces also combined to intensify the pressure for change. Some of these forces are discussed here.

Attitudes regarding desirable family size have been changing. Many more women (including married women with children) have been going to work outside home.

Since the late 1940s as increasing proportion of women have been attending colleges due to non-discriminating laws, a broader range of colleges and universities have begun enrolling women at all degree levels. More women going to college are now taking business-related courses as well. This trend seems likely to continue, especially in light of increased legal and social pressures for equal access to all educational opportunities for both sexes, and for less stereotyping in curriculum materials "appropriate" males and females jobs or male and in vocational counselling.

Other things being equal, people will choose careers that are consistent with the beliefs about themselves. The generalization of a male "managerial model" however, contributes to the mistaken belief that women cannot be successful in management. Many recent researches indicate that women as a group tend to be successful managers posing characteristics, attitudes, and temperament more commonly associated to men in general.

The women's movements have contributed significantly to changing perceptions. It may be emphasized here that differential action for women is not an attempt to bring all women into responsible positions in organizations. The goal is to raise the consciousness levels of both women and men to create conditions that give a fair change to think about their interests and unfold their potentials.

Technological changes have also both encouraged and facilitated the energy of more women into the labour force. In the workplace itself, advances in technology have reduced subsequently the number of jobs requiring great physical strength or sustainence.

Therefore, the Human Resource Management perspective of women and work needs a greater attention of policy makers and work designers in terms of Human Resource Management Policy issues coupled with contingency management approach. Since the entry of female workforce in most of the organizations is inevitable, we have no choice other than designing suitable Human Resource Management strategies giving representation to gender in organization theory.

Bibliography

Abernathy, W.; Clark, K. and Kantrow, A Industrial Renaissance : Producing a comparative future for America., Basic Books, New York, 1983.

Adams, J.S., Towards an understanding of,inequity, J. Abnor Soc. Psychol. 1963, 67, 422-36.

Alagh, Y.K., Women's World: Women and Development. Mainstream, July, 1989.

Allport, G.W., Vernon, P.E. and Lindgey, G. Study of Values (rev. ed). Boston : Houghton Miffin, 1951.

American Sociological Review, 33 : 499-517.

Annapoorni, A study of professional socialization of women medical and nursing students in medical colleges, unpublished Ph.D dissertation, Madurai Kamraj University Press, 1929.

Baig, T.A., Indian Women Power., S. Chand and Company Pvt.. Ltd., Delhi, 1972.

Baig, T.A. (1976), Indian Woman Power. New Delhi : S Chand and Co., Sharan, R. (1985), Indian Women Workers, Cosmo Publication, New Delhi.

Bailyn, Lotte (1978), Accommodation of.work to family, in Rapoport, R. and Rapoport, R.N. (ed.) Working Couples. London, Wiley., 159-71.

Bakke, E. Concept of the social organization. In modern organization theory (ed.) M. Haire, New York: John Wily, 1959.

Banerjee, N.K. (1995), Grassroot empowerment (1975-1990): a discussion paper occasional paper, No. 22, CWDS, New Delhi.

Bardwick, J.M., Women in Transition, Harvester Press, Bringhton, 1980.

Baruch, G.K., Barnett, R.C., and Rivers, C. (1985) Lifeprints : New Pattern of Love and work for Today's women. : McGraw Hill : New York 1985.

Beardwell Ian & Len Holden (1994), Human resource management - a contemporary perspective, Macmillan India Ltd.

Becker, Howard S. (1960), Notes on the concept of commitment, American Journal of Sociology, 66: 239-47.

Biddle, B.J. and Thomas, E.J. (ed.) (1966), Role Theory:Concept and Research, New York : Wiley.

Boulding, J., General Systems theory:The skeleton of science, Management Science, 2,3, April 1956, 197-208.

Bramham, I., Human Resource Planning, I.P.M., London, 1989.

Brayfield, A.H. and Crockatt, W.H. Employee attitude and employee performance., Psychological Bulletin, 1955, 52, 396-424.

Broedling, L.A. Relationship of internal, external control to word motivation and performance in an expectancy model, Journal of Applied Psychology, 1975, Vol. 60, No. 1, 65-70.

Burke, P.J. and Reitzes, D.C. (1991), An Identity Theory Approach to Commitment, Social Psychological Quarterly, 54(8) : 239-51.

Caplow, T. Sociology of Work, Prentice-Hall, Englewood Cliffs, 1954.

Caplow, T., Sociology of Work, Mc-Graw-Hill, New York, 1954.

Chaturvedi, Geeta., Women Administration in India, A study of the socio-economic background, Jaipur, RBSA Publication, 1985.

Clegg, S.R., Hardy, C., and Mord, W.M, Handbook of Organization Studies, Sage Publication, London, New Delhi, 1996.

Cofer, C.N. and Appley, M.N. Motivation theory and research A Wiley International Edition, John Wiley and Sons Inc., 1964.

Deaus, K. and Emseviller, T. Exploration of successful performance on sex linked tasks what is skill for rule is luck for female, Journal of Pers. Soc. Psychol, 1974, 29, 80-85.

Deckard, B.S, The Women's Movement, Harper and Row, New York, 1979.

Deshpande, A., Invisibility of Women's Labour, Mainstream, July 1989.

Drucker, P.F., An Introductory View of Management, Harper College Press, New York, 1977.

Dube, S.C. (ed) (1977), India Since Independence, Vikas Publishing House, New Delhi.

Evan, M. William, Organizational theory structure, systems and environments, Wiley Interscience Publications, John Wiley and Sons Inc, London : 1976.

Feldman, Summers, S. and Kiesler, S.B, Those who are number two try harder, The effect of sex on attribution of causality. J. Person Soc. Psychol, 1974, 30: 846-55.

Fleishman, E.A, A relationship between incentive, motivation and ability level in psychomotor performance, J. Exp. Psychol., 78-81.

Foote, Nelson N. (1951), Identification the Basis for a Theory of Motivation, American Sociological Review, 26: 14-21.

French, Elizabeth, G., Effects of interaction of achievement motivation and intelligence on problem solving success, American Psychologist, 1951, 12, 399-400.

Frieze, I.H., Women's expectatios for and causal attribute of success and failure. In social psychological perspective in achievements (eds) Madvich Tangui and Hoffman. New York: Holl, Rinchard & Winstin,

1975.

Gadgil, D.R. (1965), Women in the Working Force in India, Asia Publishing House, Bombay.

Ghosh, Ratna and Douglas, R., Social Change and Education in Canada, Harcourt Brace Jovanovich : Toronto, 1981.

Government of India, Fourth World Conference on Women, Beijing 1995, country report, Department of women and child development, Ministry of Human Resource Development, New Delhi, 1995,

Greenberger, E. and Goldberg, W.A. (1989) Work, Parenting and Socialization of Children, Development Psychology, 25 (1) : 22-35.

Greenberger, E. and O'Neil, R. (1990), Parents Concerns about their Child's Development : Implication for Fathers and Mothers Well-Being and Attitudes toward Work, Journal of Marriage and the Family, 52 : 621-35.

Greenberger, E. and O'Neil, R. (1993), Spouse, Parent, Worker : Construction of Adults well-being, Developmental Psychology, 29(2) : 181-97.

Guest, D. Personal and HRM : Can you tell the difference, Personnel Management, January, 1989.

Gulford, J.P., Psychometric Methods, Tata McGraw Hill Co. Ltd, Bombay-New Delhi, 1971.

Gullahorn, J.E., Psychology and Women in transition, John-Wiley, New York, 1979.

Gupta, R.L. (1969), Women's Role in Promoting their Cause, Report, Central Institute of Research and Training Press, New Delhi.

Harmon, L.W. (1970), Anatomy of career commitment in women, Journal of Consulting Psychology, 17 (1) : 77-80.

Hate, C.A. (1969), Changing Status of Women, Post-Independence India, Allied Publishers Pvt. Ltd., Bombay.

Herman, J.B., Dunham, R.B. and Hulin, C.L., Organizational structure, Demographic characteristics and employee responses. Organizational Behaviour and Human performance, 1975, 13, 206-32.

Herman, J.B. and Hulin, C.L. Studying organizational attitudes from individual and organizational frames of reference, Organizational Behavior and Human Performance, 1972, 8, 84-108.

Herzberg, F. Work and the Nature of man, World Publishing Company, Chicago III, 1966.

Herzberg, F.B. Mauser and Snyderman, B.B, The motivation to work. New York : Wiley, 1959.

Hisrich and Brush, Women Entrepreneurs, Lexington, Massachusetts, 1985.

House, W.C., Actual and percieved differences in male and female expectancies and minimal goal lends as a function of competition, J. of Personality, 1974, 42, 493-509.

Hunter, M., The Changing family : Comparative perspective, John Wiley and Sons, New York, 1981.

Hunter, M., Changing Family : Comparative Perspective. John Wiley and Sons ; New York, 1981.

Huse, E.F. and Bowditch, J.L. Behaviour in organization. Addison Wesley Publishing Company- Inc. Reading, Mass. California, London : 1973.

Ivancevich and Matteson (1980) In Arnold, J :, Robertson, I.T. and Cooper, C.L. (ed.). (1995). Work Psychology - Understanding Human Behavior in the Work Place Macmillan, New Delhi.

Jaggar, A. M., Feminist Politics and Human Nature, Rowman and Allanheld, Totowa, N.J., 1983.

Jaiprakash, I. (1986) Women, Work and Work Commitment — A Review of Some Relevant Issues, Indian Journal of Applied Psychology, 23 (2) : 58-64.

Jaiswal, R.P, Professional Status of Women, Rawat Publishers, Jaipur; 1993.

Joe, V.C., Review of the internal external control construct as a personality valuable. Psychological Reports, 971, 88; 619-640.

Kalarani, Role Conflict in Working Women, Chitra Publications, New Delhi, 1976.

Kanter, R.M. (1968), Commitment and Social Organizations :

Kanter, Rosabeth Moss. (1968). `Commitment and Social Utopian Communities'. American Sociological Review, 33: 499-517.

Kanter, Rosabeth (1972) Commitment and Community Communes and Utopia in Sociological Perspective Combridge, NA : Harward University Press.

Kapadia, K.M. (1958)., Marriage and Family in India. :Oxford University Press, Bombay.

Katz, D., Maccoby, N., Gurin, G. and Floor, L.G., Productivity Supervisions and Morale Among Railroad Workers. Ann Arbour, University of Michigan, Survey Research Centre, Institute for Social Research, 1951.

Kelley, J., Organizational Behavior, Home Wood III, Irwin, 1969.

Kessler, R.C. & Mc Rae James A. Jr. (1982). The effect of wives employment on the mental health of married man and women.

American Sociological Review, 47, 216-227.

Khanna, G. and Varghese, M.A. (1978). Indian Women Today. New Delhi : Vikas Publishing House Pvt. Ltd.

Knowles, W.H. Human relations in industry : Research and concepts California Management Review. Vol.1, No. 1, Fall 1958, 87-105.

Kohn, M.L. and Schooler, C. Occupational experience and Psychological Functioning. An assessment of reciprocal effects., American Sociological Review, 1973, 38, 97-118.

Korman, A.K. Towards an hypothesis of work behavior. Journal of Appl., Psychol. 1970., Vol. 54, No. 1, 31-41.

Krech, D. Gutchfield, R.S. and Ballachey, E.L. The individual in Society. McGraw Hill, New York : 1962.

Kumari, S. Women workers in unorganized sectors of India, Indian Management, Oct. 1972.

Lawler, E.E., and Porter, L.W., The effect of performance on job satisfaction. Industrial Relations, Vol. 7, No. 1, 1967, 20-28.

Lawler, E.E., Motivation in Work Organization, Monterey. Calif. Brooks/ Cole, 1973.

Lefcourt, H.M. Internal external control of refreshment : A Review Psychological Bulletin, 1966, 65, 206-220.

Lefcourt, H.M., Recent Developments in the Study of Locus of Control. In B.A. Maher (Ed.). Progress in experimental Research in personality, Vol. 6, New York: Academic Press, 1972.

Lewin, K. Dembo, Tamara, Festinger. L. and Sears, P.S. Level of Aspiration. In Hunt, J. Mc V (Ed.) Personality and Behavior Disorder 1944. Vol. 1, New York : Ronalod Press.

Littman, R.A., Motives, History and Causes, In Jones. M.R. (E.d.) Nebraska Symposium on Motivation, 1958. Lincoln : University of Nebraska Press. pp. 114-168.

Maslow, A. Motivation and Personality, Harper and Row, New York, 1964.

Maslow, A.H., A theory of human motivation. Psychological Review, 1943. Vol. 50, 370-396.

Matteson, M.T. Mc Mohan, J.T. and Margaret Mc Mohan Sen Differences and Job Attitudes : Some unexpected findings, Pyschological Reports, 1974, 35, 1333-1334.

Mc Gregor, D., The Human side of Enterprise, McGraw-Hill, New York, 1960.

McShane, S.L., Canadian Organization Behaviour, Irwin Boston, 1992.

Mies, M. (1980)., Indian Women and Patriarchy : Conflicts and Dilemmas of Students and Working Women. Concept Publishers, New Delhi.

Muthaya, B.C. Level of aspiration and intelligence of high achievers and low achievers and in the scholastic field. J. Psychol. Research 1962. 6, 146-149.

Myrdal, A. And Klien, V. (1968)., Woman's Two Roles, Routledge & K. Paul, London.

Nock, S.L. & Kingston, P.W. (1990)., Time with Children—the impact of couples work time commitment, Social Forces, 67 (1) : 59.

Noditch, Murray, P. and Demaw, T., Locus of Control and Competence. Journal of Personality. Dec. 1975, Vol. 43, No. 4.

Pleck, Joseph H. (1985), Basic Patterns of family work and paid work in working wives / working husbands, Sage Publications

Prakash, G., After colonialism : Imperial Histories and Post Colonial Displacements, Princeton University Press, Princeton 1995.

Ramanamma, A. (1979)., Graduate Employed Women in an Urban Setting. Dastane Ramachandra and Co, Pune.

Rani, K. (1976)., Role Conflict in Working Wives, Chetana Publications, New Delhi.

Rantalaiho, L. and Heiskanen, T., Gendered practices in working life, Macmillan, London, 1977.

Report of the committee on status of women in India (1974), Towards Equality. Department of Social Welfare, Government of India, New Delhi.

Rexroat, C. and Shehan, C. (1987). The family life cycle and spouses time in housework, Journal of Marriage and the family, 49 : 737-750.

Roby, Pamela., Women in the work place, MA. Schenkrnan Cambridge, 1981.

Rotters. J.B., External Control and Internal Control. Psychology Today, 1971, 5, 37-59.

Rotter, J.B. Generalized expectancies for internal versus external control of reinforcement. Psychological monographs. General Applied, Vol. 80., No. 1, 1966.

Safilios-Rothschild, C. (1970) The Influence of the Wife's Degree of Work Commitment upon Some Aspects of Family Organization and Dynamics, Journal of Marriage and the Family, 32 : 681-91.

Saunders, George B. and Slantzon, J.L., Personality and Influencing factors in decision making. Organizational Behavior and Human Performance 1976, 15, 245-256.

Saxena, Pradeep Kumar (1991)., Profile of Urban Women Workers. Manpowers Journal, 27 (3) : 21-399.

Scarr, S., Phillips, D. & McCartney, K. (1989)., Working mothers and their familles. American Psychologist, 44 (11): 1402-1409.

Sharma, A. Management and Job Performance, Gian Publishing House, New Delhi, 1987.

Sharma, Kumud (1989). Shared Aspirations, Fragmented Realities Contemporary Women's Movement in India— Its Dialecties and Dilemmas, Occassional Paper, November 12, CWDS, New Delhi 1989.

Sharan, R. (1985). Indian Women Workers. Cosmo Publishers, New Delhi.

Sikula, Andrew, F. Values and Value Systems : Importance and Relationship to Managerial and Organizational Behaviour. Journal of Psychol : 1971, 78, 277-286.

Sinha, J.B.P., Work Culture in Indian Context, Seth Publications, New Delhi, 1987.

Spurlock, J. and Robinowitz, C.B., Women's Progress, Promises and Problems -- Women in Context : Development and Stresses, Plenum Press : New York 1990.

Srinivas, M.N. (1978), The Changing Position of Indian Women, Oxford University Press.

Stagner, R. Perception : Applied Aspects. In the psychology of industrial conflict', John Wiley & Sons Inc, New York. 1956.

Stead, B.A. Women in Management, Prentice Hall, Englewood Cliffs, 1978.

Storey, J. Developments in the Management of Human Resources: Basil Blackwell : Oxford 1992.

Storey, J., New Perspective on Human Resource Management Routledge : London, 1989.

Stryker, Sheldon (1968), Identity Salience and Role Performance, Journal of Marriage and the Family, 4, : 558-64.

Stryker, S. & Richard T. Serpe. (1972), Commitment and Community: Communes and Utopios in Sociological perspective, Cambridge: Harvard University, Press.

Stryker, S. and Serpe, Richard T. (1982), Commitment, Identity, Salience and Role Behaviour, 199-218, in Ickes, W. and Knowles, E. (ed.) Personality, Roles and Social Behaviour, New York : Springer Verlag.

Tavris, C. & Wade, C. (1984), The longest war; sex differences in perspective. New York : Harcourt Brace, Jovanovich.

Taylor, Debbie (1992). Women, Work and Domestic Responsibility in

Huamn Societies - a reader (eds). Anthony Giddens, Polity, U.K. 1992.

Taylor, Ronald, N. Age and experience as determinants of managerial information processing and decision making performance. Academy of Managment, Journal. Vol. 18, No. 1, March 1975, 78-81.

Taylor, W.F., Scientific Management, New York : Harper, 1911.

Tolman, E.C. Principles of purposive behavior. In S. Koch (Ed.) Psychology : A study of a science. (Vol. II), New York : Mc Graw Hill, 1959, pp. 92-157.

Venkatarathnam R., Medical Sociology in an Indian Setting, Macmillian, Madras, 1979.

Vitels, M.S., Motivation and Morale in Industry. New York : Morton 1953.

Vroom, V.H. ,Work and Motivation : John Wiley & Sons, Inc. New York : 1964.

Watson, T. Management, Organization and Employment Strategy, Routledge and Kegan Paul, London, 1986.

Welsch, Harold P. and La Van H. (1981), Inter-relationships between Organizational Commitment and Job Characteristics, Job Satisfaction, Professional Behaviour and Organizational Climate, Human Relations, 34(12): 1079-89.

Whyte, F.W., Money and Motivation , Harper and Row. Inc., New York : 1955.

Index